Megan Daniels

Addictions
Become
Eternal

CONTENTS

INTRODUCTION

Anything in life is capable of becoming an addiction. Addictions have been many and varied throughout the history of mankind. Modern societies, characterized by a multitude of dependencies and inter-dependencies of men, machines and technological innovations, appear to create a vast reservoir of potentially threatening and hitherto unknown to man possibilities of developing addictive patterns of behavior. Thus, addictions have become a crucial problem that afflicts millions of individuals and disrupts the lives of their families, friends and associates costing large amounts to their employers and to health systems and charitable foundations.

Addiction or dependence has been defined as a state in which a person is unable to stop engaging in a behavior because of strong physical, psychological and social reasons. Thus, an addiction is essentially an 'excessive appetite': a repetitive behavior that is subject to powerful motivational forces. Addiction has also been defined as a repetitive habit pattern that increases the risk of financial and physical problems. Addictive behaviors are often experienced subjectively as 'loss of control' - the behavior continues to occur despite volitional attempts to abstain or moderate use. These habit patterns are typically characterized by immediate gratification (short-term reward), often coupled with delayed, deleterious effects (long-term costs). Attempts to change an addictive behavior (via treatment or by self-initiation) are typically marked by high relapse rates. The key features of an addictive behavior can be considered as a compulsion or strong desire to engage in the behavior; an overwhelming priority or salience being given to the behavior; an impaired capacity to control the behavior; distress if prevented from carrying out the behavior; and a detrimental effect on the individual, the family and society at large.

As you are starting to read our e-book, assuming and hoping that this unorthodox preamble will not surprise you, we would like to express to you our heartfelt thanks for honouring and obliging us as co-authors by downloading it on your personal electronic device your PC, laptop, Android, iPhone or iPad. We hope this book will prove to be useful to you as a free addition to your bibliography if you are a student attending a relevant University module or you are simply interested in learning more about the subjects covered in this book.

Going beyond the interested university, college or high school students we certainly hope that members of the larger public, as parents or interested individuals, will find this book useful. As co-authors we hope that your decision to download our book justifies our joint decision to add our book titled '***Addictions: An Eternal Human Condition***' to the already existing English language bibliography on 'Addictions'.

In the four parts of our book we present and succinctly analyse and assess four specific dependencies focusing on alcohol, gambling (betting), substances and tobacco. Earlier defined as addictions and now as 'use disorders', these dependencies entail both narcotic and stimulant substances as well as the *'fortune chasing'* behaviours in the form of compulsive, pathological gambling (betting and gaming), which in our opinion constitute the four most significant *'eternal human conditions'*.

Throughout human history, on a global scale, these four types of *'human conditions'* have been and continue to be adversely affecting the physical and psychological health (including the loss of life) of countless millions of individuals adding to them and their families unbearable financial burdens along with the loss of social status and integrity. The continuous tragic reality which has intensified in the last few decades is that as they encompass very large numbers of youths and adults, they constitute heavy burdens to societies and Nations across the Globe creating serious and obviously, up to now, hard to deal with and control *'social problems'*.

The above stated realization underlines dramatically, viewed within the context of the pathology and the devastating effects on individuals and society as a whole, our choice to focus in the four major topics of our book. We hope our choice is justified when viewed in the perspective of the devastating numbers and the colossal volumes of suffering from dependence (addiction) and 'use disorder' relating to alcohol, to narcotic and stimulant drugs, to nicotine contained in tobacco and, going beyond substances, to behaviors such as gambling, betting or *'interneting'* (spending uncontrollable amounts of time 'on-line' using P.C.'s, IPads or smartphone android devices).

During the last few decades on a global scale and with increasing frequency in recognition of the magnitude of the problems a vast number of Colleges and Universities are offering one or more modules in various degree specialities focusing on 'addictions'. Indeed, several hundred Universities are offering undergraduate and post graduate Master level and selectively doctoral level degrees focusing on 'addictions'.

We assume that College and University students as well as interested members of the general public are already aware of the existence of a plethora of academic level textbooks and popular books on the subject of 'addictions'. We close this brief introductory section noting that the title of our book expresses our view and our understanding of 'Addictions' as 'an eternal human condition' and we add this book to the existing bibliography hoping it will be useful to College and University students as well as to interested members of the general public on a global scale.

PROLEGOMENA

Examining the subject of 'addictions' with a sufficient dose of socio-psychological and philosophical sobriety, it will easily emerge and will be equally easy to discern that humans, throughout history, have always had the tendency to become 'addicted' to one or more of a multitude of dependency producing substances and behaviors.

The Merriam Webster dictionary classic definition of addiction was '*a strong inclination to do, use, or indulge in something repeatedly*'. When the term is used in modern periods to describe persons exhibiting a pathological condition, Merriam Webster defines addiction as '*a compulsive, chronic, physiological or psychological need for a habit-forming substance, behavior, or activity having harmful physical, psychological, or social effects and typically causing well-defined symptoms (such as anxiety, irritability, tremors, or nausea) upon withdrawal or abstinence: the state of being addicted*'.

Rosenthal and Faris in their article titled: '*The etymology and early history of addiction*' present an interesting diachronic, etymological study of addiction as it appeared in Latin in the early Roman Republic. Carrying their analysis through to our times they note that the word constitutes an auto-antonym, i.e. a word with opposite conflicting meanings. Etymologically the word has a Greek origin (it is a synthesis of the Greek word '*ἀντί*' meaning 'against' and the Greek word '*ὄνομα*' meaning 'name'). An auto-antonym (also called a contronym or, a 'Janus' word simulating the two-faced Roman god) is a word with multiple meanings, one of which is defined as the reverse of one of its other meanings (*Merriam Webster* online).

The origin of the word 'addiction' stems etymologically from the Latin root '*dicere*' meaning to '*say or to speak*' from which the addition of the proposition '*ad*' produced the term '*Addicere*' forerunner to the English term 'addiction'. As the authors note 'addictions' from early Roman Empire times to early English times have been used to describe both positive and negative attachments to persons, ideologies and habits. In our era it is almost universally accepted that when we use the term 'addictions' we are almost exclusively referring to 'pathological' dependence on substances and behaviors which enslave an individual and are detrimental to his physical and mental health and, extending it to gambling, to his financial status (Rosenthal & Faris, on-line 2019).

Highlighting the current co-existence of '*positive addictions*' as exhibitions of healthy types of individual and group behaviors in contrast to '*negative, pathological addictions*' Rosenthal and Faris bring forth the term '*positive addiction*' used by psychiatrist William Glasser to describe a healthy positive behavior, like running or meditation, that strengthens the individual's functioning. According to Glasser, engaging in either of those behaviours regularly, at a dosage of about an hour a day, will produce a non-critical, transcendental state of mind. Glasser identified that pleasurable mental state as the 'positive addiction' (Glasser, 1976).

Modern human societies characterized by the dizzying evolution of high technology and the diffusion to billions of users on a global scale of related devices as tools of work and leisure, are experiencing new and unforeseen types of '*addictive*', pathologically dependent behaviors. As the relevant statistical data show, some very modern 'addictions' have been added to the classic substance abuse and dependencies such as, dependencies to virtual reality games, and the use and 'abuse' of the internet through endless 'surfing' by children, adolescents and adults.

For social and behavioral scientists, sociologists, social workers, psychologists, psychiatrists, '*addictive*' is considered to be any behavior that the individuals are unable to control or mitigate and much more to stop, as social and psychological factors render them weak and at the same time '*captives-victims*' of their frail, uncontrollable pathological behavior. Many critics hold the same view for excessive and uncontrollable dependence on the so-called 'positive addictions'.

Each and every human being, a boy, a girl, a man, a woman, constitutes a unique existence endowed with the DNA helix inherited from their parents. As we grow up, through socialization and acculturation processes, each one of us develops a distinct personality and character internalizing a multitude of attitudes towards other persons, institutions and realities prevailing in the sub-culture and the main culture of our societies. Motivated by personal reasons such as curiosity or the pursuit of pleasure derived from adventure seeking, or drawn into and encouraged by peers, an individual may start using narcotic or stimulant substances or may engage in behaviours which can ultimately become 'addictions'.

In many societies, not in the very distant past, such behaviours have been dismissed by a section of public opinion as problems characterizing certain types of individuals or members of certain sub-cultures. As such they are not deemed worthy of the attention and the intervention of Authorities, Charitable Institutions and Society in general despite the obvious and detrimental damaging psychological and physical effects to individuals and families. However, it should be noted that when the numbers of those using and abusing 'addictive' substances or engaging in 'addictive' behaviours swell in parallel swelling fashion with comorbidity characteristics such as the amounts of money involved and threat to physical and psychological health, societies are faced with what social scientists conventionally have defined as 'social problems' needing the intervention of State Authorities and Charitable Institutions.

This book is the result of the combined effort of father and daughter as the two co-authors, who, as practitioners, are not strangers to the subject matter of substance use disorders and behavioural 'addictions'. Indeed this book in not their sole creative contribution as authors on these subjects as is shown below in a brief glimpse at their individual, published work written mostly in Greek.

Georgios in the late 1960's and in the 1970's was an academic-practitioner and a full member of the American Psychological Association (APA – Division 50 then known as *'Society of Psychologists in Substance Abuse'*). He served in a variety of consulting and managerial posts in the American States of Massachusetts and Rhode Island in drug addict outreach, rehabilitation and community reinstatement self-help, State and Federal Government funded programs. Georgios is currently *a Life Member of the APA, Division 50 – Society of Addiction Psychology*.

Georgios returned to Greece shortly before the end of 1978 accepting the position of Manager for Industrial and Public Relations with Goodyear, Hellas, S.A., a wholly owned subsidiary of the Goodyear Tire and Rubber Company of Akron, Ohio, USA. Soon thereafter Georgios took notice of the intense Greek Mass Media revelations of a fast rising drug abuse problem among Greek youths as the decade of the 1970's was coming to its end.

As an experienced professional with drug abuse problems in the USA and in his new position as manager of Industrial and public relations for Goodyear Hellas, S.A., Georgios saw the possibility of gaining positive responses to a Goodyear initiative within the general framework of Corporate Social Responsibility by making a practical contribution to the Greek society. He wrote a pamphlet on drug abuse and addiction and sought the approval of Goodyear's Board of Directors and the necessary funds to print and disseminate his pamphlet free of charge to strategically significant individuals and organizations in Greece.

Aiming to secure the dual benefit on the one hand of helping Greek parents and Greek Authorities understand the intensifying problems of drug abuse and dependency and on the other hand upgrading Goodyear's public image, he succeeded in securing the authorization of the Goodyear Hellas, S.A. Board of Directors and the necessary funds to print and disseminate several thousands of his pamphlet titled: "*Drug Addiction – A Hot Problem of Our Times*" (in Greek the title was: «*NAPKOMANIA: Ένα 'καυτό' Πρόβλημα της Εποχής μας*»).

The pamphlet was published early in 1980 under the author's name with an especially emphatic subheading note: *'a goodwill public offering of Goodyear Greece'*. A few months later a second printing followed as a result of the public's demand for the pamphlet and the accolades of the Greek Mass Media to Goodyear for its contribution in understanding and confronting the rapidly rising drug abuse problem.

Thousands of copies were distributed free throughout Greece to Goodyear customers through the corporation's chain of tire selling shops. Packages containing dozens of copies of the pamphlet were provided to Primary and Secondary School Head Teachers, Principals and Directors and their staff members, to Police and Hospital Directors and their personnel, to Health officials and their staffs on Central, Regional and prefecture levels and to charity NGO's.

Almost two decades later, after leaving his management post with Goodyear Hellas, Georgios was a professor at the Department of Management of the University of Macedonia and also a well-established management consultant to National and Multinational corporations operating in Greece. As the problems relating to alcohol and substance dependencies among young and adult Greeks were intensifying having held the copyright to his pamphlet he proceeded to add a section on alcohol abuse to the original pamphlet published by Goodyear and changed its title to: *"Dependencies: Alcohol and Drugs"* (in Greek: *«ΕΞΑΡΤΗΣΕΙΣ: Αλκοολισμός- Ναρκωτικά»*).

Georgios succeeded in having his new pamphlet sponsored, published and distributed free in dozens of thousands of copies successively:

By The Army General Staff, Hellenic Armed Forces in 1997;

By the KONSUM one of Greece's largest Supermarket chains in 1998;

By the National Bank of Greece Employees Health Fund in 2002; and

By the Kozani, Western Macedonia Co-Operative Bank in conjunction with the Western Macedonia Hellenic Police Directorate in 2005.

Georgios as the author of the pamphlet having the copyright to his work, chose not to receive any royalties for the successive publication and free country-wide distribution of dozens of thousands of copies of his pamphlet (http://piperopoulos.blogspot.com/p/blog-page_27.html).

Subsequently as an academic-practitioner Georgios authored a book titled *"Dependencies and Deviations"* (in Greek: «Εξαρτήσεις και Αποκλίσεις») dealing with the major contemporary social problems. Published initially by the University of Macedonia Press in 2002, the book as a self-edition by the author was marketed in three subsequent editions: in 2004, 2006 and 2008.

Anastasia-Natasha's dissertation submitted in fulfilling the requirements for her Master's in Health Psychology at the Department of Psychology of Surrey University was titled: '*Stock market trading: a compulsive gambling behavior with potential psychological and health problems*'. A Journal article of her dissertation was published in the quarterly Journal of the Hellenic Psychiatric Association's PSYCHIATRIKI in 2004 (Piperopoulou, 2004).

After receiving her Master's degree she volunteered her services as a psychologist in the drug addict therapeutic rehabilitation program (18+) of the Attica Psychiatric Hospital of Greece.

From January 2003 to November 2009 Anastasia-Natasha was employed as a psychologist at the 414 Army Psychiatric Hospital of the Hellenic Ministry of National Defence providing telephone psychological counselling services to Hellenic Army and Air Force personnel and was simultaneously serving as a member of the *'crisis intervention team'* providing support to families of victims of Armed Forces personnel. Furthermore, she also served as a member of the medical team providing psychological services to Armed Forces personnel who were admitted and hospitalized at the 414 Army Psychiatric Hospital.

In 2010, having fulfilled all relevant academic requirements and having submitted her Doctoral Thesis to the Department of Psychology of Panteion University of Athens titled: *'Psychological factors of stock market trading addiction and compulsive gambling behaviour'* (in Greek: *'Ψυχολογικοί Παράγοντες της Εξάρτησης από Χρηματιστηριακές Συναλλαγές και Τυχερά Παιχνίδια')* was awarded her Doctoral degree with the highest distinction (grade 10) and was named the valedictorian during the June 2010 ceremony of conferring Doctoral Degrees.

THE 'RAISON D'ÊTRE' OF THIS BOOK: SUBSTANCES AND BEHAVIOURAL ADDICTIONS

On a global scale, throughout the last decades of the 20th century and with increased intensity during the first two decades of the 21st century, the audio-visual and printed Mass Media of Communication, have been presenting to their audiences countless news stories, serials, in-depth focused articles and editorials on personal and family dramas relating to various 'Addictions'. Such stories present and highlight loss of lives and loss of large amounts of monies, from fateful dependencies to a variety of the known 'substance addictions' and to insurmountable addictive behaviours relating to various forms of 'gambling, betting and gaming'.

Starting in the early months of 2019 and intensifying during the summer and towards the end of the year, the Mass Media of Communication especially in Europe and North America brought forcefully to the forefront of public awareness the intensifying problems of all 'addictions' presenting, as we will briefly show below, statistics that are staggering, or as the familiar English language colloquial expression goes, *'mind blowing'*...

At this point we will ask for your understanding as in the following few pages we will present a select number of significant Mass Media of Communication articles and editorials focusing in an alphabetical order on the four parts of our book, namely alcohol, gambling-betting-gaming, substances and tobacco published in 2019 in the year before the publication of our book in 2020.

We will start the presentation of our selection of Mass Media highlighted stories taking a brief glimpse to the Global use of alcohol and drugs and noting that 164 million people (68% of them, or in real numbers 111 million, were males) who had an alcohol or drug use disorder in 2016 (Ritchie and Roser, 2020).

According to a World Health Organization (WHO) Global Status Report on Alcohol and Health released in September 2018, some 3 million people died during 2016 as a result of harmful use of alcohol (that number represented 1 out of every 20 deaths recorded that year). Alcohol increases the risk of death in diseases related to liver, cardiovascular problems and some types of cancer. Deadly car and motorcycle accidents and physical violence incidents caused while under the influence of alcohol are also contributing factors to the 3 million annual deaths (alcohol is the leading worldwide risk factor for deaths of males aged 15-19. 6.2% of all male deaths are attributable to alcohol. The respective number is 1.1% for females) (WHO, 2018).

Gambling and betting legally in casinos, in Main Street betting-shops and on-line using PC's, laptops, IPads and mobile phones (as well as the classic practice of illegally placing bets with neighbourhood book-makers) is globally a main feature in the audio-visual and printed Mass Media of Communication exposing personal and family dramas relating to huge losses of money.

Assessments of the real amounts of money involved in legal and illegal gambling-gaming and betting are not so readily available. However, we bring to your attention a relevant Encyclopedia Britannica article titled 'Gambling' (and with an alternative title 'Betting') authored by Dan Glimne, according to which a rough estimate of the amount of money legally wagered annually on a global scale is about $10 trillion, while the total sums of illegal money exchanging hands in a global scale may exceed the legal amount (Glimne, Encyclopedia Britannica).

As noted in a World Atlas article by John Miaschi based on data from H2 Gambling Capital, titled 'Countries That Gamble The Most' using as a benchmark amounts of money gambled and lost per adult in US dollars globally, the 10 leading countries in descending order are given below. The population of each country reflects the 2015 UN estimated data for each of the 10 leading countries: (1) Australia (pop. 23,401,892) ($1,288.00) -- (2) Singapore (pop. 5,076,700) ($1,174.00) -- (3) Ireland (pop. 4,467,854) ($588.00) -- (4) Canada (pop. 34,108,752) ($568.00) -- (5) Finland (pop. 5,351,427) ($553.00) -- (6) Italy (pop. 60,340,328) ($517.00) -- (7) Hong Kong (pop. 7,024,200) ($503.00) -- (8) Norway (pop. 4,858,199) ($448.00) -- (9) Greece (pop. 10,444,289) ($420.00) -- (10) Spain (pop. 45,989,016) ($418.00) (Miaschi, 2017).

The world's 15 biggest gambler Nations On February 9, 2017 in descending order were: Australia, Singapore, Ireland, Finland, United States, New Zealand, Canada, Norway, Italy, Britain, Iceland, Cyprus, Sweden, Denmark and Malta (The Economist, 2017).

Daryl Charman, a Las Vegas expert, in his article titled '*Which Countries Gamble the Most*' on the on-line *Bingo.co.uk*, lists in descending order the following five countries: Australia, Singapore, Ireland, Canada and Finland (Charman, 2019).

Michael Hawthorne in his article for the on-line *Jackpot.co.uk* titled '*10 biggest gambling countries of the world by the numbers*', notes that on-line gambling has become an important part of worldwide gambling. His list in descending order includes the United Kingdom, Australia, China (where online gambling and land based casinos are prohibited) and Macau (which for the Chinese is their Las Vegas, Nevada gambling paradise), India, Ireland, Finland, Singapore, USA, Canada and Italy (noting that some 800,000 Italians have a gambling addiction) (Hawthorne, 2019).

The November 2018 research study of the UK Gambling Commission brought forth the fact that 14% of young people aged 11-16 years old, a statistic which translates in real numbers to some 450,000 youths, gambled their own money in the week preceding the week examined by the researchers (UK Gambling Commission Survey, 2018).

A year later in the Gambling Commission's report published in October, 2019 it was reported that the percentage for the same age category of 11-16 year old youths dropped to 11% (which translates in real numbers to a total of 350,000 youths) in England, Scotland and Wales (UK Gambling Commission Survey, 2019).

However, the significant reality remains that both the 2018 and 2019 annual reports assessed that some 55,000 eleven to sixteen year olds in the UK were problem gamblers. The NHS opened its first clinic for young people addicted to gaming and gambling early in October 2019. The new Centre for Internet and Gaming Disorders launched at the same time as the children and young person's gambling addiction service went live. The 'Centre for Internet and Gaming Disorders' is part of the National Centre for Behavioural Addictions, which also supports those who are addicted to the internet (UK National Health Executive, 2019)

Internet-dependency appears to be rising globally as Technology marches on by 'leaps and bounds' and literally billions of people have access to and regularly use social media. The age levels at which adolescents and children have access to mobile phones and tablets in North America and Europe has been decreasing year after year during the first two decades of the 21st century. In a Guardian news story on 1st November, 2019 Nancy Joe Sales reported that in the US some 53% of 11 year olds have their own smartphone and the percentage jumps to 69% when they get to be 12 years old (The Guardian, Nov. 1, 2019).

BBC reporter Zoe Kleinman bringing forth on February 4, 2020 the findings of the report of UK's media regulator **Ofcom** highlights the fact that 50% of UK's 10 year olds owned a smartphone in 2019. The report notes that 24% of 3 and 4-year-olds had their own tablet, and the number jumps to 37% for 5-7 year olds. According to Ofcom 48% of girls aged 5-15 played online games, compared with 71% of boys. Boys spent twice as much time playing, appx. 14.5 hours per week, compared to 7.5 for girls (Kleinman, 2020).

In January 2020 the UK Gambling Commission formally announced that effective on April 14, 2020 gambling businesses will not be allowed to permit consumers to use credit cards when gambling. Between August and November 2019 the UK Gambling Commission held a public consultation on online gambling, gaming machines and social responsibility measures. In the UK 24 million people gamble and some 10.5 million of those gamble on line. According to the UK Gambling Commission 22% of those using credit cards when gambling on line are classified as 'problem gamblers' and some 800,000 consumers who use credit cards to gamble are using money they do not have (UK, Gambling Commission 2020).

Gambling and betting, verifying the adage that 'the House always wins', almost routinely result in the loss of small and, not too seldom up to vast amounts of money which for individuals with a compulsive habit of pathological dependence place them and their families

in severe financial straits creating significant and very often insurmountable personal and family dramas.

Concluding our process of highlighting problems related to gambling-betting-gaming we will proceed noting that pathological dependency on drugs results in a multitude of health complications and in some instances leads to the loss of life. In the case of pathological gamblers beyond the loss of money many are lead to the desperate act of attempting to and some ultimately and literally succeed in ending their addiction by putting an end to their personal existence through the act of suicide.

Some 8,200 deaths involving the use of one or more illicit drugs were reported in the European Union in 2017 with the United Kingdom and Germany counting for almost half of them. It should be noted that over 92 million people in the European Union aged 15-64 reported that they have used illicit drugs during their lifetime. For most of them cannabis was the main drug, but many have also used cocaine, amphetamines, ecstasy and other drugs (European Drug Report 2019 – online -pdf).

At the '*New World*' side of the Atlantic Ocean, alarming was the impressive number of 30.5 million Americans aged from 12 years onwards listed as current illicit drug users in 2017. According to the Report of the US Department of Health & Human Services, Substance Abuse and Mental Health Services Administration (SAMHSA), about 140.6 million Americans aged 12 or older were current alcohol users, 66.6 million were 'binge' drinkers and 16.7 million were heavy drinkers in the past month before the publication of this USA National Report (USA, SAMHSA 2018).

In 2017 over 70,000 drug related overdose deaths were recorded in the USA (47,600 of the overdose deaths, namely 67.8% of all drug overdose deaths involved licit and illicit opioids usage). This number exceeded the number of lives lost in car accidents or gun related homicides recorded in the same year in USA (Scholl et al., 2019).

During 2019 various opioid producing pharmaceutical giants as well as distributors of legally prescribed opioid drugs were in the process of dealing with literally thousands of lawsuits brought against them by individuals, families, Municipalities and States. In this respect, according to an October 18, 2019 article in the Wall Street Journal three giant pharmaceutical distributor companies, namely McKesson, AmerisourceBergen and Cardinal Health, were discussing settlements to individuals, families and Public Entities amounting to the impressive sum of some 18 billion dollars (Randazzo, S., 2019).

In a parallel vein to the Wall Street Journal article noted above, in October, 2019 a New York Times article under the title 'Drug Giants Close In on a $50 Billion Settlement of Opioid Cases' reported that under the mounting numbers of Lawsuits, 3 of the Nation's largest drug distributors as well as two manufacturers of opioid drugs were held responsible for the *'epidemic'* of over 400,000 overdose deaths in the last two decades in the USA (Hoffman, J., 2019).

Zeroing in on the protagonists held ethically and legally responsible for the opioid deaths *epidemic* in the 20 years between 1999 and 2019 as reported in an October 17, 2019 article in VOX, Purdue Pharma, the maker of OxyContin, had tentatively agreed to pay as much as $12 billion to settle lawsuits it faced for its role in the opioid crisis (Lopez, G., 2019).

In the European Union, in the U.S.A. and the rest of the Globe countless millions of individuals regularly use prescription drugs (including opioids) administered by their physicians in dealing with their emotional and physical problems. This legally approved practice exacerbates the 'eternal' human condition of 'Addictions' which emerges globally as an immensely more sinister daily reality in addition to illicit drugs used by 'addicts', i.e. persons who currently are classified as individuals facing a substance use disorder (SUD).

Summing up the above it should become clear to our readers that the case of legally prescribed opioids resulting in 'addiction' and ultimately some 400,000 deaths in the United States of America during the 20 year period between 1999 and 2019 came to the forefront and received wide global publicity in the Mass Media during 2019. According to CNN Health Report and the Report by the American Centers for Disease Control and Prevention among all the States those of Alabama, Arkansas, Mississippi and Tennessee had the highest opioid prescription rates in 2017 (CNN Health 2004).

In the year 2017, the States with the highest rates of death due to drug overdose were West Virginia (57.8 per 100,000), Ohio (46.3 per 100,000), Pennsylvania (44.3 per 100,000), the District of Columbia (44.0 per 100,000), and Kentucky (37.2 per 100,000) (Scholl L, et al 2019).

States which showed statistically significant increases in drug overdose death rates from 2016 to 2017 included Alabama, Arizona, California, Connecticut, Delaware, Florida, Georgia, Illinois, Indiana, Kentucky, Louisiana, Maine, Maryland, Michigan, New Jersey, New York, North Carolina, Ohio, Pennsylvania, South Carolina, Tennessee, West Virginia, and Wisconsin (Scholl, et al., 2019, op. cit.).

We will close this section of our co-authored treatise which we have characterized as 'the 'raison d'être' of this book: substance addictions and addictive behaviors' with a very brief reference to the World Health Organization (WHO) Report on tobacco published in the summer of 2019. According to this Report it is estimated that on a Global scale 1.1 billion people are smokers and around 80% of them live in low-and-middle-income countries.

On 26 July, 2019 the World Health Organization (WHO) Report on the Tobacco epidemic noted that it kills over 8 million people each year! More than 7 million of the 8 million victims are 'active' smokers. An additional 1.2 million victims are the so-called 'passive smokers' or non-smokers who lose their lives as a result of inhaling the smoke exhaled by smokers. According to the Report 80% of the World's 1.1 billion smokers live in low-and middle-income countries. In the fourth part of our book, where we will present and discuss the addiction to tobacco smoking, we will also highlight the incidents of serious lung injuries and several deaths reported in Europe and North America as a result of the current trend of countless tobacco smokers using e-vaping in their attempts to free themselves from their nicotine dependency (WHO Tobacco Report, 2019).

A PORTRAIT FROM LIMBO

Alcohol, cannabis, pills: ephemeral 'escape' to…nowhere!

He was a thin, pale, reserved, pleasant lad who was experiencing the exuberance and the trial of adolescence … As a new summer free of school burdens time started unfolding his need to escape from the suburban boredom found a way out with the help of his small group of 'revolting' friends.

The common denominator, the underlying bond of friendship among the group members was the pervasive, uncertain, unspecified but real sense of 'lack of genuine communication with their parents'. The group's purpose did not aim to explore the how's and why's of their daily realities, but rather to pursue, without proper and honest effort, the eradication of that pervasive sense of boredom and 'escape' through experiencing thrills which bring ephemeral but intensely sensual meanings, smoking cannabis, swallowing a pill!…

At other times, here in this very same city, 'escape' meant finding the means to leave poverty behind, while engaging in a frantic rush to secure a decent day's income. 'Escape' was note fuelled by the lack of the freedom to enjoy life but by the lack of financial resources that would make possible the right to enjoy some free time, the right to enjoy life…

Nowadays this city is a different, significantly changed but not necessarily a better world to live in as countless families have access to improved financial resources. Socio-economic success translates in the accumulation of more and more consumer products squeezed into modern asphyxiating dwellings in this noisy, ceaselessly awake, painfully inhumane city…

The need for 'escape' started in late childhood and early adolescence, experienced at first as what seemed to be an unintentional, unwelcome exhibition of parental indifference … It emerged as the father struggled with overtime efforts to secure the financial resources that would buy consumer goods, a larger house, a new car, a new SUV, which would impress friends and neighbours while the working mother also contributed towards those goals...

The skinny teenager did not understand the meaning and could not perceive the value of acquiring and adding an SUV to the house parking lot or more house ornaments of bohemian porcelain and marble; but he understood and treasured memories of some years back of the sweet warmth of his mother's embrace, the transfer of love when his father patted his little head ... As a child he understood and deeply enjoyed a walk in the park when while holding on his parents arms he would spring into the air and with one, two, three of their steps, hop, he would land having made a giant step ...

While his parents drawn into the prevailing life-work-style were struggling to improve their socio-economic status the skinny little child metamorphosed to an adolescent started to miss those precious simple things that money never could and never will manage to buy...

And there, while he entered puberty and the family added ornaments of crystal and bohemian porcelains, the caresses, the strolls and the giant steps were abandoned giving way to what appeared to be parental indifference...

That's how the skinny teenager saw it...

When a child looks upward, the world of parents and other older relatives seems like a fascinating, hard to reach, inaccessible, magical entity... Children engage in phantasies of suddenly and magically acquiring long legs and long arms, now able to reach the grown-ups, lovingly hug them and whisper in their ears:

'Hey guys what's this all about? Did you forget me?'

The struggle to amass financial means needed to buy and own the symbols of success in our modern societies devours the parental time and vitality, steals love and other emotions abandoned in the process of accumulating inanimate, consumer goods money can buy...

Fatigue sets in and emotionally neutralizes the parents exhausted by overtime work for creating in the child's soul, the inexorable need to 'escape' from an unbearable reality...

As the child becomes an adolescent the need to 'escape' from emotionally unbearable family realities takes on a variety of shapes and forms: impersonal-irresponsible sex, anti-social behavior, cigarettes, alcohol, cannabis, pills, and even 'shooting dope'!

Another summer evening after the end of the school year and the skinny, pale, reserved-though pleasant adolescent joined his group of friends, sat at the park bench and once more engaged in the substance produced hallucination of an ephemeral 'escape' to ...nowhere!

PART ONE – ALCOHOL

Preamble

The unorthodox preamble to PART ONE of this book devoted to discussing alcohol in a worldwide historic overview of its use and abuse, was suggested by Natasha who prompted her co-author (and father) Georgios to make public his fascinating personal experience with alcohol consumption when he first went to America as a foreign student in the summer of 1960.

Natasha and her brother Panagiotis (Panos) as teenage high school students growing up in Greece received concerted and systematic parental guidance in the use of alcohol, which in Greece from the 1960's to today has had a MLDA (Minimum Legal Drinking Age of 18). During such family discussion sessions they heard their father and their late mother recount personal experiences and incidents with friends consuming alcohol during their late adolescent and early adult years. Natasha and Panos were particularly impressed with their father's fascinating memories of his experience with alcohol consumption during his first summer in America and specifically his experience of being refused to be served a drink in Bennington, Vermont.

Georgios as a foreign student holding a scholarship from the Anglo-American-Hellenic Bureau of Education and a Fulbright grant was scheduled to enter his freshman year at the City College of the City University of New York in September of 1960. He arrived in New York in August, 1960 and under the auspices of the Institute of International Education he was sent to Bennington College (at that time a distinguished women's higher education institution which became co-educational in 1969) located in Bennington, Vermont. He was scheduled to take part in a so-called 'acculturation' session aimed to familiarize scholarship holding foreign students with the American culture and the American Higher Education System.

Georgios at the time was 18 years old but his facial characteristics and somatotype made him look more as being in his early twenties as were the rest of his group of fellow foreign students participating in the Bennington College acculturation program. Several American students who acted as 'hosts' and several of the foreign students during their first Saturday evening went out to a local Bennington restaurant for dinner. It was at that occasion that Georgios confronted the problem of being under the MLDA age which at the time in the State of Vermont was the 21st year. Georgios missed his glass of wine which he could have at his homeland Greece at age 18 and had to settle in the Bennington restaurant with a soda drink....

In their next outing, the mixed group of American and foreign students considering Georgios' age problem, crossed the border and entered the neighbouring New York State where MLDA was 18 and Georgios could have and enjoy his first glass of wine on American soil...

Flabbergasted by the experience of the drinking age difference within two New England region US States Georgios raised the issue with his American professors at Bennington College. He was informed that there was no uniform Federal MLDA but each State had the right to set its own drinking age limits. He posed the seemingly naïve question relating to the danger of consuming alcohol at an earlier age than permitted in their home State of Vermont, Georgios learned that mostly during weekends countless teenagers would drive across the State border, many engaging in binge drinking, which had the end result of some losing their lives and many others sustaining serious bodily injuries as a result of accidents caused by driving intoxicated.

In a special section of PART TWO we will take a brief glimpse at the historic 'Alcohol Prohibition Laws' in the USA which failed to succeed in their mission and were repealed by the 21ˢᵗ Amendment on Dec. 5, 1933 allowing each State to set its own MLDA alcohol consumption laws. What emerged after that repeal were legal discrepancies between neighbouring States across the whole USA leading to countless serious, and sometimes fatal, automobile accidents by youngsters engaging in 'binge drinking' in a neighbouring State with MLDA of 18 instead of 21.

The passage of the 26ᵗʰ Amendment to the Constitution of the United States on July 1, 1971 lowered the legal voting age from 21 to 18 years of age. Using this as a benchmark 30 US States lowered the MLDA to 18, 19, or 20. By 1982, only 14 states still had an MLDA of 21. In 1984 the enactment of the National Minimum Drinking Age Act prompted States to raise their legal age for purchase or public possession of alcohol to 21 or risk losing millions in federal highway funds. Facing serious loss of Federal funds by 1988, all 50 states had raised the MLDA to 21.

On a global scale as given in the 2014 World Health Organization (WHO) 'Global Status Report on Alcohol and Health' the United States and 11 other countries have the highest MLDA in the World at age 21 while in over 60% of the 190 countries studied the majority have MLDA at 18 or 19 and there are 16 mostly Muslim countries which have a universal ban on alcohol consumption. This book is written and published in 2020 when the USA has the MLDA limit at age 21 and Canada at age 18 in Quebec, Manitoba and Alberta and 19 for the rest of the country. The US New England States of Vermont, Maine, New Hampshire and New York border with Quebec (WHO, Alcohol Report 2014).

Most readers of our book have heard the popularised adage that 'History repeats itself' as it has been noted in a number of variations since the 5ᵗʰ century BC and the work of the Greek Historian Thucydides and up to the 20ᵗʰ century and the work of the Spanish born Harvard educated American classic philosopher and author George Santayana...

In 1960 when Georgios first visited Vermont where the State MLDA age was 21, local youths had to cross over to New York where the MLDA was set at 18 to have a drink or to go on binge drinking. Nowadays teenagers from Vermont who cross the National borderline between USA and Canada in order to be able to have an alcohol containing drink, because of the change in US MLDA laws, are joined by teenagers who live and grow up in the State of New York.

Bringing the adage to everyday reality, as humans have difficulty learning from experiences Georgios and Natasha, raise a simple but pointed question:

'Are there official estimates on how many American teenagers cross the American – Canadian border daily and especially on weekends most of them to enjoy a drink and some, unfortunately, to engage in binge drinking with all the dangers driving under the influence of alcohol entails?'...

1 ALCOHOL USE AND ABUSE FROM ANTIQUITY TO OUR TIMES

If you ever decide to launch a personal search for historical sources relating to the discovery and patterns of consumption of alcohol by humans you will encounter a plethora of scientific resource materials and of Mass Media of Communication popular news articles and editorials. You, as countless of other interested readers, will be fascinated by the available information covering the journey of fermented and later distilled alcoholic drinks from prehistoric times to the present. In your search you will also come across and read a variety of accounts associated with a time-old dilemma of human societies which appears in the following form: recognizing and permitting their members to consume alcohol containing drinks and experience the related pleasant effects, while simultaneously introducing norms, rules and regulations aiming to curtail the ultimately catastrophic effects of short and long term overconsumption and abuse of alcohol.

In this respect we bring to your attention, in addition to other resources you may locate, a lengthy article authored by Andrew Curry published in the February, 2017 issue of the National Geographic with the catchy, popular title: *'Our 9,000-Year Love Affair With Booze'* and a subtitle which notes: *'Alcohol isn't just a mind-altering drink: It has been a prime mover of human culture from the beginning, fuelling the development of arts, language, and religion'*. The article brings forth in a fascinating, reader absorbing style significant historic and cultural facts.

The word alcohol originates from the Arabic word 'al kuhul' (al kohl) which was adapted to English a few centuries ago and rendered globally ever since as 'alcohol'. It is considered as an irrefutable assumption that fermented grain, fruit juice and honey have been used by humans several thousand years ago to produce alcoholic drinks (containing ethyl alcohol or ethanol).

Archaeological evidence and unearthed artefacts are often used as approximate milestones of the historic times ancient people started consuming alcoholic drinks. In this context it is estimated that the Chinese were making wine from rice, honey and fruit at around 7,000 years BC, early evidence of grape wine was located at the Zagros Mountains of Iran dating to 5,000 BC and at 3,500 BC large scale brewing and winemaking appeared in Mesopotamia and Egypt.

In ancient Greece an early alcoholic beverage was called *mead* and it was the product of fermentation of honey with water while occasionally fruits and spices were also infused in the drink, (mead is known in Greek as 'υδρόμελο' or 'υδρόμελι' combining the word for water – 'ύδωρ' and for honey – 'μέλι').

Spyridon Marinatos, a noted Greek archaeologist, has suggested that seafaring members of the Minoan empire of Crete brought wine making from Egypt to Crete and the Greek mainland before the Minoan Empire was subdued by mainland Greek forces around the 15th century BC (Marinatos, 1959).

During that epoch Phoenicians and later Greek seafaring merchants introduced the various Mediterranean people to 'viniculture' (the term refers to the cultivation of grapes especially those used to produce wine) or 'viticulture' (the term refers to the agricultural practices of growing grape vines). As large scale cultivation of grapes and meticulous fermentation produced a variety of types and qualities of wine, the Greeks created a special type of clay jars called the *amphora* (in Greek 'αμφορεύς') for the safe land and sea transportation and sale of wine.

The Hebrew term 'yayin', the English word wine, the Roman 'vinum', the modern Italian and Spanish vino, are all referring to the yeast in the process of fermentation of grapes and relate etymologically to the ancient Greek word 'oinos (in Greek 'οίνος'). It should be noted, however, as you may already have heard the word if you have visited Greece and surely you will hear it when you do visit that modern Greeks also use for wine the word 'krasi' (in Greek 'κρασί').

The usefulness of wine, its positive effect on the mental and emotional state of the consumer appears in Psalm 104:14-15 of the Old Testament (the Psalm is given as 103:14-15 in the Greek Orthodox numbering system). According to Biblical tradition, King David (who lived and reigned circa 1035 to 975 BCE) is usually referred to as its author: *"You cause the grass to grow for the livestock and plants for man to cultivate, that he may bring forth food from the earth, and wine to gladden the heart of man, oil to make his face shine and bread to strengthen man's heart"* (Bible Gateway Psalm 104: 14-15).

In the middle of the last millennium BC, in 5th century Athens the term *symposium* (in Greek 'συμπόσιο' which etymologically means drinking together with friends) denoted the gathering of friends after dinner engaging in discussions of a variety of intellectual subjects. One of Plato's dialogues bears the title '*Symposium*' (in Greek 'Συμπόσιο') in which some of the distinguished and important participants were Socrates, Agathon, Alcibiades, Aristodemus, Pausanias, Aristophanes, and Glaucon. For the Greeks (and later on for the Romans) strong types of wine should be drank after being mixed with water at a ratio of one part wine and three parts water. Dionysus (in Greek Διόνυσος) the Greek God of grape harvest, wine, festivity, pleasure and wild frenzy exhibited in the famed 'Dionysian cult, Dionysian mysteries and orgies' was the son of Zeus and Semele, the daughter of mythical Cadmus the founder and first King of Thebes (later on Bacchus appeared as the Roman rendition of Dionysus).

In the New Testament John makes reference to the first miracle by Jesus when as a guest with His mother and disciples He discovers that the hosts have run out of wine and He transforms water into excellent quality wine John 2:6-10 *"Nearby stood six stone water jars, the kind used by the Jews for ceremonial washing, each holding from twenty to thirty gallons. Jesus said to the servants, "Fill the jars with water"; so they filled them to the brim. Then he told them, "Now draw some out and take it to the master of the banquet." They did so, and the master of the banquet tasted the water that had been turned into wine. He did not realize where it had come from, though the servants who had drawn the water knew. Then he called the bridegroom aside and said, "Everyone brings out the choice wine first and then the cheaper wine after the guests have had too much to drink; but you have saved the best till now."* (Bible Gateway, John 2: 6-10).

Be it as it may the reality remains that ever since antiquity and the discovery of the pleasant effects of the liquid product of fermented grapes or other fruits known as wine and brewed grains such as malted barley, corn, rice and wheat known as beers, societies have had to cope with the realities both of modest use and careless overconsumption of alcoholic drinks. Later on when the distilling process was discovered (as distilled drinks contain much higher levels of alcohol) the problems of use and abuse intensified and continue to be in the forefront of societal concern.

1.1   THE ALCOHOL PROHIBITION ERA IN AMERICA (1920-1933)

Closing this section we feel obliged to our readers to make a very brief mention of the historic period known as *alcohol prohibition years* in the USA (roughly 1920 to 1933). The US Congress lending an ear to demands posed by women's groups, such as WCTU, the Women's Christian Temperance Union, some mainly Protestant religious groups as well as the outspoken Temperance Movement, voted and passed in January 1919 the 18th Amendment which went into effect in January 1920. The Amendment enforced a total ban on the production, distribution, sale and consumption of alcoholic drinks.

The philosophical, sociological and ethical foundations which lead to the birth and application of the American 'Prohibition era' were based on the assumption that alcohol was the basic root of many of society's ills and the force behind all social problems. Andrew Volstead, at that time Chairman of the House Judiciary Committee, engineered the passage of the National Prohibition Act (which relating to his name was commonly referred to as the Volstead Act). The *Veto* against the Volstead Act exercised by President Woodrow Wilson was overridden on October 27, 1919 by the Congress and on October 28, 1919 by the Senate and America entered the historic *'Prohibition Era'*. Accounting for that historic period there exists a plethora of books, scientific research articles as well as Media articles and editorials (Rorabaugh, 2018).

As it turned out, prohibition intensified the rise of crime as organized gangs of mobsters (*Al Capone* became a world-wide familiar name of a criminal involved in illegal production and sale of alcoholic drinks). It should be noted that while Women's groups played key roles leading to the creation and passage of the 18th Amendment, Women's groups spearheaded by the Women's Organization for National Prohibition Reform led the drive for voting and passing of the 21st Amendment. In March 1933, shortly after taking office, President Franklin D. Roosevelt signed the Cullen-Harrison Act, which amended the Volstead Act, permitting the manufacturing and sale of low-alcohol beer and wines. A few months later, in December 1933 the 21st Amendment was ratified and brought the end to the National ban on production and sale of alcoholic drinks. The 18th Amendment holds the historic characteristic of being the one and only Amendment in the United States Constitution which had secured ratification and was later repealed (Encyclopaedia Britannica, the editors, Eighteenth Amendment).

1.2 CURRENT GLOBAL REALITIES ON ALCOHOL CONSUMPTION

Alcoholic drinks in any typical serving vary in the content of alcohol they contain. The USA National Institute on Alcohol Abuse and Alcoholism provides the following as a general point of reference: the 12 fl. ounces of a can or bottle of beer contain 5% of alcohol by volume, a typical glass of 5 fl. ounces of table wine contains 12% of alcohol by volume and a shot of distilled spirits, in a typical glass of 1.5 fl. ounce contains about 40% of alcohol by volume. The above measures of alcohol content may vary among different brands of drinks and are increased in all alcoholic drinks designated as 'fortified' (NIAAA online).

According to the World Health Organization (WHO - 2017) report: *'The WHO European Region has the highest proportion in the world of total ill health and premature death due to alcohol. The European Union is the heaviest-drinking region in the world, with over one fifth of the European population aged 15 years and above reporting heavy episodic drinking (five or more drinks on an occasion, or 60g alcohol) at least once a week. Heavy episodic drinking is widespread across all ages and all of Europe, and not only among young people or those from northern Europe'* (WHO Fact sheet, Alcohol 2017).

On a global scale, as reported in a November 2018 World Health Organization Report, some 3 million deaths every year, representing 5.3% of all deaths result from harmful use of alcohol. Beyond the deaths and other health problems related to the habitual abuse of alcohol, excessive alcohol consumption also results in significant financial and social losses to individuals, families and societies *(WHO Fact sheet, Alcohol 2018).*

Viewed in a global scale, alcohol consumption is characterized by significant as well as interesting geographical differences. The geographic regions across North Africa, sub-Saharan Africa, the Eastern Mediterranean region, and southern Asia and the Indian Ocean are regions which have very high rates of abstention representing large populations of the Islamic faith. Alcohol consumption appears in very high levels in the developed world and especially in Europe, the USA and Canada as well as in Argentina, Australia and New Zealand (WHO Global Status Report on Alcohol and Health, 2018).

Alcohol intake across Europe is highest in the Czech Republic, Lithuania, and Moldova. Western European countries including Germany, France, Portugal, Ireland, and Belgium are only slightly behind the Eastern European countries while in France in 2010 almost 95% of the adult population reported drinking alcohol in the preceding year. Globally, comparing men and women alcohol consumption is clearly higher among men (Hannah Ritchie and Max Roser, 2020).

2 THE CONTEMPORARY DEFINITION: ALCOHOLISM AS AN 'ALCOHOL USE DISORDER' (AUD)

The American Psychiatric Association's *'Diagnostic and Statistical Manual of Mental Disorders'*, Fifth Edition (DSM-5) published in 2013 has combined the DSM-4 (1994 edition) categories of *alcohol abuse* and *alcohol dependence* into a single disorder named *alcohol use disorder* (AUD) with mild, moderate and severe sub-classifications.

If you are aiming to diagnose your personal problem with alcohol consumption or that of a relative, friend or associate the US National Institute on Alcohol Abuse and Alcoholism suggests that you ask the following 11 questions concerning alcohol use in the last 12 months:

- Had times when you ended up drinking more, or longer than you intended?
- More than once wanted to cut down or stop drinking, or tried to, but couldn't?
- Spent a lot of time drinking? Or being sick or getting over the aftereffects?
- Experienced craving — a strong need, or urge, to drink?
- Found that drinking — or being sick from drinking — often interfered with taking care of your home or family? Or caused job troubles? Or school problems?
- Continued to drink even though it was causing trouble with your family or friends?
- Given up or cut back on activities that were important or interesting to you, or gave you pleasure, in order to drink?
- More than once gotten into situations while or after drinking that increased your chances of getting hurt (such as driving, swimming, using machinery, walking in a dangerous area, or having unsafe sex)?
- Continued to drink even though it was making you feel depressed or anxious or adding to another health problem? Or after having had a memory blackout?
- Had to drink much more than you once did to get the effect you want? Or found that your usual number of drinks had much less effect than before?
- Found that when the effects of alcohol were wearing off, you had withdrawal symptoms, such as trouble sleeping, shakiness, irritability, anxiety, depression, restlessness, nausea, or sweating? Or sensed things that were not there?

The evaluation of responses according to the NIAAA is that positive answers to 2 or 3 questions constitutes a mild Alcohol Use Disorder; 4 to 5 positive answers describes moderate cases while 6 and more positive answers describe persons severely affected by their alcohol consumption patterns (NIDA – Alcohol Use Disorder*)*.

2.1 IDENTIFYING 5 SUBTYPES OF ALCOHOLICS OR (AUD) ALCOHOL USE DISORDER INDIVIDUALS

As far as Americans are concerned an interesting answer to the classic question which usually has been posed in the form of 'is there a typical alcoholic' came as a news release from the US on June 28, 2007 from an epidemiological study conducted by scientists at the US National Institute on Alcohol Abuse and Alcoholism. The findings showed that there are 5 different subtypes of AD based on their clinical characteristics, namely:

The Young Adult subtype represents 31.5 percent of U.S. alcoholics. These are young adult drinkers, with relatively low rates of co-occurring substance abuse and other mental disorders, a low rate of family alcoholism, and who rarely seek any kind of help for their drinking.

The Young Antisocial subtype represents 21 percent of U.S. alcoholics. They tend to be in their mid-twenties, had early onset of regular drinking, and alcohol problems. More than half come from families with alcoholism, and about half have a psychiatric diagnosis of Antisocial Personality Disorder. Many have major depression, bipolar disorder, and anxiety problems. More than 75 percent smoked cigarettes and marijuana, and many also had cocaine and opiate addictions. More than one-third of these alcoholics seek help for their drinking.

The Functional subtype represents 19.5 percent of U.S. alcoholics. Typically they are middle-aged, well-educated, with stable jobs and families. About one-third have a multigenerational family history of alcoholism, about one-quarter had major depressive illness sometime in their lives, and nearly 50 percent were smokers.

The Intermediate Familial subtype represents 19 percent of U.S. alcoholics. They are middle-aged, with about 50 percent from families with multigenerational alcoholism. Almost half have had clinical depression, and 20 percent have had bipolar disorder. Most of these individuals smoked cigarettes, and nearly one in five had problems with cocaine and marijuana use. Only 25 percent ever sought treatment for their problem drinking.

The Chronic Severe subtype represents 9 percent of U.S. alcoholics. They are comprised mostly of middle-aged individuals who had early onset of drinking and alcohol problems, with high rates of Antisocial Personality Disorder and criminality. Almost 80 percent come from families with multigenerational alcoholism. They have the highest rates of other psychiatric disorders including depression, bipolar disorder, and anxiety disorders as well as high rates of smoking, and marijuana, cocaine, and opiate dependence. Two-thirds of these alcoholics seek help for their drinking problems, making them the most prevalent type of alcoholic in treatment (Howard B. Moss, Chiung M. Chen, Hsiao-Ye Yi, 2007).

3 TREATING ALCOHOLICS: MUTUAL SUPPORT GROUPS, PSYCHOTHERAPY AND ANTI-ALCOHOL DRUGS

Publishing the results of the research team's extensive research in the Lancet on June 22, 2019 under the title *'Global alcohol exposure between 1990 and 2017 and forecasts until 2030: a modelling study'*, lead author Jacob Manthey reported that on a global scale some 237 million men and 46 million women suffer from alcohol-related disorders, with the highest rates in Europe (15% and 3.5%, respectively, for men and women) and North America (11.5% and 5%). The research team is forecasting that by 2030 half of all adults worldwide will drink alcohol, and almost a quarter will binge drink at least once a month. The report also notes that by 2030 two countries will change their current ranking places as the Chinese will be drinking more alcohol than the Americans (Manthey, J., Shield, K.D., et al 2019).

The case of dealing with alcoholics, AUD individuals, resembles that of all other addicted persons. Indeed, it is not what family members and friends are ready and willing to do to control or fully alleviate their relative's dependency on alcohol but it is when the individuals will decide to do something about their problem. When alcoholics, AUD persons, decide to seek help, both for them and their families, the crucial question was and continues to center on the means available for helping them gain control of their drinking habits or ultimately to achieve total abstinence from alcohol.

Historically, the two basic treatment choices relate to in-patient and out-patient treatment including in some instances admission to Hospital detoxification units. Abrupt abstinence from alcohol may pose serious health dangers for an alcoholic, an alcohol use dependent (AUD) individual. In such cases the individual is referred to a short term alcohol detoxification hospital unit. However, the detoxification process, commonly referred to as 'detox', does not constitute a proper treatment modality but a necessary intervention in life threatening circumstances.

In-patient clinic or hospital treatment of AUD individuals in specialized residential, medically supervised units or in residential rehabilitation programs staffed by recovered alcoholics where medical consultants are available entail substantial financial commitments which individual alcoholics and their families cannot afford for lengthy periods of time. Furthermore, for financially less fortunate persons and for persons unwilling to commit themselves to the structured residential rehabilitation programs but needing support their families are unable to provide another modality has been the so-called half-way houses for treatment of alcohol dependent persons. Half-way houses were readily visible after the WWII and during the 1970's but progressively faded-away in the following decades (Straussner, 2004).

Systematic clinical findings and long term accumulated empirical evidence suggest that dealing with both the understanding of causality and the application of treatment the so-called 'biopsychosocial' model is fast replacing the classic biomedical model which has traditionally dominated the general field of addictions. The biomedical model viewed the addictions as manifestations of disturbance in the inflicted individuals' neurophysiological or biochemical processes. The biopsychosocial model originally proposed by George L. Engel, a physician-specialist in internal medicine with psychotherapeutic training, posits that biogenetic as well as psychological and sociocultural factors contribute to addictive behaviour and must be taken into account at both the understanding/ prevention and treatment efforts (Engel, 1997; 1981).

Currently the prevalent treatment modality is not so much the in-patient residential type which may last from 3 or 4 weeks up to six months, but rather the out-patient modality which in many instances may combine participation in AA meetings, psychotherapeutic treatment offered to individuals and families and medically supervised administration of special anti-alcohol drugs.

On a global scale the available approaches in treating individuals with AUD are:

- 'Self-help' types of therapeutic treatment such as the classic Alcoholics Anonymous '12-Step' program which aims at achieving, one day at the time, total abstinence from consumption of alcohol containing drinks;
- Counselling and psychotherapeutic treatment such as Cognitive Behavioral Therapy (CBT);
- Medically supervised administration of one or more of the officially approved by relevant Health Services (FDA in the USA, NHS in the UK, National Health Systems in EU) anti-alcohol drugs.

3.1 ALCOHOLICS ANONYMOUS (THE AA 'MUTUAL-SUPPORT' FELLOWSHIP)

It was in 1784, as the 18th century was coming to its end, that a Pennsylvania physician named Benjamin Rush described the loss of control of alcohol consumption and its potential treatments recommending practicing the Christian religion. In practical terms Rush's treatment included a series of remedial measures such as experiencing guilt and shame; pairing alcohol with aversive stimuli; developing other passions in life; following a vegetarian diet; taking an oath to not drink alcohol, and sudden and absolute abstinence from alcohol. Through the 1800s and early 1900s, the temperance movement laid the groundwork for mutual help organizations, and the notion of excessive alcohol use as a moral failing (Witkiewitz1, Litten and Leggio, 2019).

Drawing on information publicly available at various sites of the global Alcoholics Anonymous fellowship we are informed that AA had its beginnings in 1935 at Akron, Ohio, as the outcome of a meeting between (the reader should note the avoidance of providing surnames of AA participants) Bill W., (Bill Wilson, born William Griffith Wilson, 1895-1971) a New York stockbroker, and Dr Bob S., (Dr Robert Smith, born Robert Holbrook Smith, 1879-1950) an Akron surgeon. Both had been hopeless alcoholics and prior to that time, Bill and Dr Bob had each been in contact with the Oxford Group, a mostly non-alcoholic fellowship that emphasized universal spiritual values in daily living. In that period, the Oxford Groups in America were headed by the noted Episcopal clergyman, Dr Samuel Shoemaker. The founders association with the Oxford Group, according to some, was responsible for the obvious spiritual orientation of AA and the reliance on Divine Province (reference to God) in helping alcoholics to recover (Alcoholics Anonymous, online, Historical data).

A second AA group took form in New York in the fall of 1935 and a third AA group appeared in Cleveland, Ohio by 1939. That same year the fellowship published a book in which most text was written by Bill, explained AA's philosophy and methods and contained the historic and ever since globally recognized '12 steps' of recovery from alcoholism.

The well-known historic AA '12 steps' on the road to recovery are shown below:

1. *We admitted we were powerless over alcohol - that our lives had become unmanageable.*
2. *Came to believe that a Power greater than ourselves could restore us to sanity.*
3. *Made a decision to turn our will and our lives over to the care of God as we understood Him.*
4. *Made a searching and fearless moral inventory of ourselves.*
5. *Admitted to God, to ourselves and to another human being the exact nature of our wrongs.*
6. *Were entirely ready to have God remove all these defects of character.*
7. *Humbly asked Him to remove our shortcomings.*
8. *Made a list of all persons we had harmed, and became willing to make amends to them all.*

9. *Made direct amends to such people wherever possible, except when to do so would injure them or others.*
10. *Continued to take personal inventory and when we were wrong promptly admitted it.*
11. *Sought through prayer and meditation to improve our conscious contact with God as we understood Him, praying only for knowledge of His will for us and the power to carry that out.*
12. *Having had a spiritual awakening as the result of these steps, we tried to carry this message to alcoholics and to practice these principles in all our affairs.* (Alcoholics Anonymous, online, Great Britain – The 12 steps of Alcoholics Anonymous).

These '12 steps' focus on the individual and his or her efforts to liberate themselves from dependency on alcohol. In the course of several decades of existence AA has developed and adopted a fellowship focused list of '12 Traditions' which serve to show how AA maintains its unity and relates to the world around it, namely the way it lives and grows. The '12 Traditions' were first put into writing in 1946 in the fellowship's international journal, the AA Grapevine and during the 1950 International Convention of AA in Cleveland, Ohio they were accepted and endorsed by the membership as a whole. The '12 Traditions' are shown below:

1. *Our common welfare should come first; personal recovery depends upon AA unity.*
2. *For our group purpose there is but one ultimate authority - a loving God as He may express Himself in our group conscience.*
   Our leaders are but trusted servants; they do not govern.
3. *The only requirement for AA membership is a desire to stop drinking.*
4. *Each group should be autonomous except in matters affecting other groups or AA as a whole.*
5. *Each group has but one primary purpose-to carry its message to the alcoholic who still suffers.*
6. *An AA group ought never endorse, finance or lend the AA name to any related facility or outside enterprise, lest problems of money, property and prestige divert us from our primary purpose.*
7. *Every AA group ought to be fully self-supporting, declining outside contributions.*
8. *Alcoholics Anonymous should remain forever nonprofessional, but our service centers may employ special workers.*
9. *AA, as such, ought never be organized; but we may create service boards or committees directly responsible to those they serve.*
10. *Alcoholics Anonymous has no opinion on outside issues; hence the AA name ought never be drawn into public controversy.*

11. *Our public relations policy is based on attraction rather than promotion; we need always maintain personal anonymity at the level of press, radio and films.*

12. *Anonymity is the spiritual foundation of all our traditions, ever reminding us to place principles before personalities* (Alcoholics Anonymous, online, Great Britain – AA Traditions*)*.

Alcoholics Anonymous has grown into a worldwide fellowship of men and women who have a drinking problem. It is a truly global organization counting over two million participants in more than 118,000 groups operating in approximately 180 Nations and its literature has been translated in a multitude of languages. Statistically its membership is made up by 62% men and 38% women. AA does not charge membership dues or fees, it is nonprofessional, multiracial, self-supporting, apolitical, and there are no age or education requirements. Membership is open to anyone who wants to do something about his or her drinking problem. Depending on the locations in each Nation where AA operates *open meetings* can be attended not just by the alcoholics but by members of their families while closed meetings are designed to be only for the alcoholics. Meetings may run daily and the alcoholic person can attend some or all of them. Once the alcoholic has decided to participate he or she is assigned 'a mentor' or a guiding more experienced recovered alcoholic (Alcoholics Anonymous, online, A.A. around the world).

The therapeutic success of Alcoholics Anonymous in helping alcoholics, individuals with alcohol use disorder to free themselves from dependency on alcohol and maintain their sobriety through their life turns out to be very hard to determine. A fundamental principle of the AA fellowship is the maintenance and protection of the anonymity of those participating in the '12 step' programs a reality which curtails objective scientific assessments of the program's success.

Lilienfeld and Arkowitz in their Scientific American article published March 1, 2011 and titled *'Does Alcoholics Anonymous Work?'* *(*Subtitled *'For some heavy drinkers, the answer is a tentative yes*) present some interesting views on the efficacy of the AA '12 step' fellowship programs. They make reference to anthropologist William Madsen's 1974 book titled *'The American Alcoholic; The Nature-Nurture Controversy in Alcoholic Research and Therapy'* in which he claimed that AA programs had 'nearly miraculous' success rates and conclude that as it emerges from relevant research AA may be helpful for many alcohol dependent people especially in conjunction with professional treatment (Lilienfield and Arkowits, 2011).

Stein and Forgione writing in the Los Angeles Times in their article published March 20, 2011 and titled *'Charlie Sheen claims AA has a 5% success rate -- is he right?'* after noting that they do not believe in much that Sheen is spouting they do admit that the 5% statistic has people talking and wondering if the massive popular program is doing that bad a job in combating alcohol abuse. The two authors note that addiction specialists cite success numbers closer to 8%-12% and they refer to a 2007 study in the journal Alcoholism: Clinical and Experimental Research which stated that those participating in the '12 Step' treatment programs had a 49.5% abstinence rate after one year, while those who were in cognitive behavioral therapy programs had a 37% abstinence rate (Stein and Forgione, 2011).

A more thorough assessment of AA effectiveness and success rates is given by Lee Ann Kaskutas in her article titled 'Alcoholics Anonymous Effectiveness: Faith Meets Science' published in the Journal of Addictive Diseases (Kaskutas, 2009).

Going beyond rates of success of AA participants remaining sober some criticisms have emerged over the years concerning the fellowship's strict adherence to the relationship of the alcoholic with God (or some Higher Power over the individual) which critics relate to the 1930's when AA was created while America was experiencing a Christian revivalist movement. AA's insistence on total abstinence and day-by-day sobriety has also drawn some criticism as the fellowship in *The Big Book* (AA's core text named so because of the thickness of the book's first edition in 1939) maintains that *"there is no such thing as making a normal drinker out of an alcoholic. Science may one day accomplish this, but it hasn't done so yet"*. More recent criticisms centre on the slang term 'the 13th Step' (beyond the AA fellowship's '12 Steps' referring to cases where men who have been sober for over a year become mentors to young alcoholic women and sexually abuse them. Obviously the Anonymity of the AA fellowship in such cases operates as a 'cover-up blanket'. Some relevant information on both of the above criticisms of AA can be found in a Sunday November 29, 2015 article in the Guardian (Stewart, 2015).

Almost as a rule Alcoholics Anonymous meetings, as do Gamblers Anonymous, Drugs Anonymous and other 12-step fellowship meetings starts with the recitation (and usually also closes) of the so-called *'serenity prayer'* attributed to Harvard University Protestant theologian Reinhold Niebuhr (Karl Paul Reinhold Niebuhr, 1882-1971, theologian and professor for more than 30 years at Union Theological Seminary). For several decades in the 20th century there were many debates focusing on the fatherhood, the creator of the *'serenity prayer'* and for those of our readers interested in familiarizing themselves with these debates we suggest an extensive article in the Chronicle of Higher Education titled 'Who Wrote the Serenity Prayer'. The most commonly encountered version of the *'serenity prayer'* is the following:

'God grant me the serenity to accept the things I cannot change; courage to change the things I can; and wisdom to know the difference.' (Shapiro, 2014).

3.2 PSYCHOTHERAPEUTIC APPROACH: COUNSELLING AND BEHAVIORAL THERAPIES

Psychological intervention in helping alcoholics gain control or fully liberate themselves from their alcohol use dependency comes in the form of individual counselling and family therapy. In the former treatment approach a trained and qualified practitioner counsels the alcoholic providing support in face-to-face sessions; in the latter approach the individuals with AUD problems as well as their family members participate in therapeutic sessions. There are various types of family therapy but in general terms they all aim at either resolving intra-family problems which may have initially triggered the individual's AUD behaviour or, vice-versa, ameliorating the individual's AUD negative impact on the lives of other family members. In engaging the alcoholics and their family members in some type of behavioral psychotherapy, a qualified psychologist/psychotherapist will analyse and present to the alcoholic his or her catastrophic entanglement in the uncontrollable consumption of alcoholic drinks.

Prevalent among behavioral therapies is the type known as Cognitive Behavioral Therapy (CBT). In its contemporary form Cognitive Behavioral Therapy (CBT) takes into account the realizations that our thoughts and thought processes *(the way we think)*, our emotional experiences *(the way we feel)* and the way we act *(our exhibited behaviour patterns)* are interrelated and basically feelings and behaviour are determined by our thoughts (we feel and behave) as our thoughts dictate.

CBT is a short term psychotherapeutic intervention (it usually involves from 4 or 6 to 14 or 16 sessions) in the course of which the trained therapist identifies the problematic, negative and dysfunctional thought processes of the individual which shape and affect his or her emotional state and exhibited behaviour patterns. Following the identification process of CBT the individual is presented with positive thought processes which when adapted and replacing the previous negative ones result in positive feelings and positive behaviour patterns.

Predecessors to modern Cognitive Behaviour Therapy (CBT) emerging after the Second World War in America and quickly spreading across the Globe have been Albert Ellis' Rational Emotive Behaviour Therapy (REBT) and Aaron Beck's Cognitive Therapy (CT). Ellis' REBT helps the individual identify and challenge self-defeating thoughts and feelings and replace them with positive more productive ones. Beck's CT proposes that the way people perceive their experiences influences their emotional, behavioral, and physiological reactions. Correcting misperceptions and modifying unhelpful thinking and behavior brings about improved reactions (Ellis, A. and Dryden, W., 1997; Beck, A. 1979).

3.3   ANTI-ALCOHOL DRUGS

The US Food and Drug Administration up to now has approved only 3 specific anti-alcohol drugs for use in alcohol use disorder (AUD) which are: **Disulfiram** (brand name *Antabuse)*; **Acamprosate** *(brand name Campral)*; and **Naltrexone,** *(brand names Revia, Vivitrol, Depade)*.

Disulfiram (brand name *Antabuse*) was the first drug to be approved by FDA as far back as 1951. On average, within about 10 minutes after an alcoholic takes disulfiram it blocks a specific enzyme that is involved in metabolizing alcohol in the human body and if the alcoholic proceeds to consume even a small amount of alcohol the effect will be that he or she will experience a variety of unpleasant symptoms which include nausea, headache, tachycardia and vomiting.

Acamprosate (brand name *Campral*) was the second in historical sequence anti-alcohol drug to be approved for use in America, Canada and Japan after it was approved and used with treatment seeking alcoholics in Europe in 1989. Acamprosate's mechanisms in affecting persons with alcohol abuse disorder are still not clear and the major common side effect is diarrhoea. The drug's overall effectiveness is less related to helping alcoholics reduce their drinking and is more related in promoting abstinence and preventing relapse in already detoxified alcoholic patients.

Naltrexone, *(*brand names *Revia, Vivitrol, Depade*) is an opioid receptor *antagonist* which works by blocking the activation of opioid receptors. Instead of controlling withdrawal and cravings, it treats opioid use disorder by preventing any opioid drug from producing rewarding effects such as euphoria. Naltrexone was approved by FDA for use initially in 1984 for the treatment of opioid dependent person*s* and was the third drug approved by FDA in 1994 for use in treating alcohol use disorder (AUD individuals). The drug was first made available and up to now continues to be available for oral administration as a pill. In 2006, twelve years after the initial FDA approval for oral administration of naltrexone, the Federal Drug Administration approved the newly developed form of naltrexone as a monthly slow release injectable drug. It is fairly well established that naltrexone reduces alcohol craving and helps reduce heavy drinking.

In addition to the above three anti-alcohol drugs approved for use in the USA by the FDA and also approved for use in the United Kingdom and Europe there is **Nalmefene** another anti-alcohol drug used in Europe but not yet approved by FDA.

Nalmefene *(*brand name *Selincro*) like **Naltrexone** is also an opioid receptor antagonist bearing similarities to naltrexone. In 2013 the drug was approved for use in Europe. **Nalmefene** has a longer half-life than **Naltrexone** and it is particularly effective in reducing 'binge type behavior' or heavy drinking days (Witkiewitz et al, op. cit. 2019).

3.4 COMBINATION OF PSYCHOTHERAPY AND ANTI-ALCOHOL DRUGS PRODUCES BETTER RESULTS

Before closing our discussion on alcohol, we will emphasize that the most appropriate and productive form of treatment of individuals with alcohol use disorder (AUD) is the one which, in accordance with the biopsychosocial model, combines some form of psychotherapy with the medically supervised use of anti-alcohol drugs.

Mutual support therapies such as Alcoholics Anonymous and other types of '12-Step' types of treatment do not encourage, nor do they discourage, the medically supervised use of drugs while participating in a fellowship program. Indeed AA suggests that peers should not intervene in the lives and actions of their peers who may be taking drugs properly prescribed by medical professionals while participating in a '12-Step' program. The same attitude of permissiveness for taking medically prescribed drugs is prevalent among psychotherapists and psychologists providing counselling and some type of Behavior Therapy including Cognitive Behavioral Therapy (CBT) who do not discourage individuals fully motivated to control their alcohol intake or succeed in achieving full abstinence.

PART TWO – GAMBLING (BETTING)

Gamble (and gambling) is defined in the Merriam Webster dictionary as to play a game for money or property; to bet on an uncertain outcome; to stake something on a contingency: take a chance.

Gamble is defined as to do something that involves risks that might result in loss of money or failure, hoping to get money or achieve success according to the Cambridge English dictionary.

Gambling, is the activity of playing games of chance for money and of betting on horses, etc. according to the Oxford Learner's dictionaries.

Dan Glimne in his article on Gambling (betting) in the Encyclopaedia Britannica defines Gambling as: 'the betting or staking of something of value, with consciousness of risk and hope of gain, on the outcome of a game, a contest, or an uncertain event whose result may be determined by chance or accident or have an unexpected result by reason of the bettor's miscalculation.'

Halliday and Fuller have suggested that a gamble may tentatively be defined as a re-allocation of wealth, on the basis of deliberate risk, involving gain to one party and loss to another, usually without the introduction of productive work on either side. The determining process always involves an element of chance, and may only be chance (Halliday & Fuller, 1974).

For Potenza and Fiellin Gambling can be defined as placing something of value at risk in the hopes of gaining something of greater value. Traditional forms of gambling include wagering in casinos and on lotteries, horse and dog racing, card games, and sporting events (Potenza, Fiellin et al, 2002).

4 GAMBLING (BETTING): FROM PREHISTORIC TIMES TO THE 21ST CENTURY

Artifacts unearthed by archaeological excavation findings, drawings on cave walls and written historical documents verify that games relating to forecasting the future, selecting directions for future activities and eventually the 'chase of fortune' in simple or more complex types and forms with underpinning of divinations have been in existence ever since antiquity.

As a pastime, appearing in a variety of forms, gambling has been present in all cultures, all periods of time, widely participated in by members of all social strata in all societies, involving people of all ages ranging from children/ adolescents to elderly persons (Fisher, 1993).

The process of chasing the good fortune was represented in ancient Greece by the goddess of luck named 'Tyche' (in Greek Τύχη) who was later identified by the Romans as 'Fortuna'. She was considered as a capricious goddess often shown winged, wearing a crown, and bearing a sceptre and cornucopia. She also appeared blindfolded and with various devices signifying uncertainty and risk. Among her monuments was a temple at Argos, where the legendary Palamedes is said to have dedicated to her the first set of dice, which he is supposed to have invented (Greek Legends and Myths, Tyche, online).

Rolling or casting the dice was a behavior encountered in ancient societies across the known ancient world initially as part of the efforts of shamans to foresee the future and then as part of gambling for fun or for money. The original forms of dice were the bones of the ankles of a hoofed animal such as a sheep or a goat. This type of bone etymologically originating from the Greek word 'astragalos' (in Greek αστράγαλος) has six surfaces, i.e. 2 rounded and four flats. When rolled this piece of bone would have to land on one of the four flat sides as it could not do so on one of the two rounded sides. With the passing of time, the ankle bones were rounded off to a square form and when rolled they could land in any one of their 6 sides. Ultimately to this new type of dice numerical values were added to each surface of the dice. The addition of an Arabic number to each side was done in such a way as adding the numbers of opposite sides would always produce the number seven, i.e. one and six, two and five, three and four (Ricky, 2000).

Gambling-gaming constituted a routine pastime for the ancient Egyptians, Greeks, Hebrews and Romans in the Western hemisphere and for the Chinese, Japanese and Indians in the Eastern hemisphere and engaged the interest not only of mature individuals but also of youth and to some extent children. Coming to our times I will kindly ask you to pause for a moment, look at many contemporary children's games. Be objective in judging what you see and you will easily realize that they involve 'luck and fortune seeking' behaviors by casting or rolling dice, pulling cards or turning a wheel which resembles the classic table roulettes on which their mothers and fathers, grandmothers and grandfathers ceaselessly place their bets hoping to win and, for most of them almost as a rule, end up not winning but losing money.

As in 2020 the year this book is published we have entered the third decade in the first century of the 3rd millennium the classic 'chase of fortune' underpinning a variety of forms of gambling and gaming is exhibiting an almost geometrical growth rate. This realization is alarming Governments and Charitable institutions not only in the industrial, financially developed Nations, but also in Nations characterized economically as developing or less well developed. In North America and Europe the amounts of money involved in both legal and illegal forms and types of gambling-gaming are approaching astronomical figures and heights.

In the European Union, according to the relevant 2017 report of the European Gaming and Betting Association (EGBA) the types of the modern form of online gambling-gaming, show that Sports betting (with 40.3%) was the most popular form of online gambling in Europe, followed by casino games (with 32.1%), lottery (with 13.3%), poker (with 6.1%), bingo (with 4.6%), and other games (with 3.6%). The share of the online gambling represents 21% of the total EU gambling market while the other 79% is land based including lotteries, casinos and bookmaker shops. The online gambling economic size, according to the above report, was expected to rise from the sum of €19.6 billion in 2017 to the sum of €24.7 billion in 2020 (EGBA, 2018).

In the United Kingdom in the middle of 2018 the Government announced that the maximum stake on fixed-odds betting terminals (FOBTs) set at that time at the amount of £100 placed every 20 seconds would be reduced to 2 pounds (BBC 2018). The reaction of the Gaming industry was strong and the leading companies indicated that such action would result in store closures and layoffs (Hancock and Hodgson, 2019).

It is a universally familiar post-card picture scene seeing a group of friends or members of a family around the New Year's dinner table engaging in a card game or some other type of game 'chasing their fortune' on the eve of a New year. On a larger scale this scene includes literally countless millions of people who will sit around a table of friends or in a casino table 'chasing their fortune' at New Year's Eve. This is a more or less romantic picture of mature and younger persons engaging in gambling and gaming. In reality there is a staggering number of people who engage themselves in gambling-gaming warming up six months before New Year's Eve, and then continuing into the semester following New Year's Eve with a feverish pursuit of luck.

On a global scale the proverbial 'pursuit of fortune and luck' expressed by gambling and gaming as an approved, legal activity is characterized by the vast numbers of persons of all ages engaging in it and the generation of huge, in some cases astronomical, amounts of profits for Governments and corporations. There are also huge amounts of unaccountable monies involved in the illegal bookmaking activities of individuals and organized gangs who operate 'in the dark'.

We have already mentioned above the Encyclopedia Britannica article titled 'Gambling' (and with an alternative title 'Betting') authored by Dan Glimne, according to which a rough estimate of the amount of money legally wagered annually on a global scale is about $10 trillion while illegal money involved may exceed this amount.

In the United Kingdom according to the Gambling Commission Report of May, 2019 the total gross gambling yield was £14.5 billion between October 2017 and September 2018. The report indicated that in the UK as of October 2018 there were 8.423 betting shops, 750 Bingo premises and 152 casinos, 183,813 gaming machines and 33,360 B2 machines (UK Gambling Commission Report, 2019).

5 FROM THE US 'WIRE ACT OF 1961' TO EU'S COMMISSION RECOMMENDATIONS OF 2014

In 1961 the US Congress passed the Interstate Wire Act of 1961, typically referred to as simply the "Wire Act," a law designed to combat organized crime. The conception and implementation of this law is often attributed to then-Attorney General Robert F. Kennedy. The Wire Act gave law enforcement agencies another weapon enabling them to put mobsters behind bars for longer sentences than previously possible under US State laws. The main objective of the Wire Act was to stop sports betting. The concern was that the integrity of contests could be compromised by the bookmaking black market. The enormous wealth created by illegal sports betting was giving organized crime power that the federal government aimed to quash. The Wire Act of 1961 made it illegal for anyone to engage in the transmission in interstate or foreign commerce of bets or wagers or information assisting in the placing of bets or wagers on any sporting event or contest, or for the transmission of a wire communication which entitles the recipient to receive money or credit as a result of bets or wagers, or for information assisting in the placing of bets or wagers (Schwartz, 2005).

In 2011, the United States' Department of Justice issued an opinion stating that the Wire Act only made internet gambling on sports illegal. It did not apply to online lottery, poker or casino games. Responding to that decision Delaware was the first State to legalize on line gambling in 2012, while Nevada and New Jersey followed in 2013. New Jersey became the third State to legalize online gambling, authorizing the issue of both online poker and online casino licenses to casinos in Atlantic City. In April 2013, the first legal online gambling site in the United States went live in Nevada. It was an online poker room called *Ultimate Poker*. By November 2013, online poker and online casinos went live in Delaware and New Jersey. In 2017 the State of Pennsylvania became the fourth and largest State to pass legislation regulating online gambling. Both online casinos and an online poker room launched in 2019.

In 2018, the *Supreme Court* overturned the Professional and Amateur Sports Protection Act (PASPA) which ignited a wave of interest across several States in authorizing sports betting, including online sports betting. In 2019 a new US Department of Justice *opinion* stated that the 1961 Wire Act applies to all bets and wagers leaving in limbo the on-line gambling in America.

The United Kingdom's *Gambling Act of 2005* created the Nation's Gambling Commission aiming to regulate and control realistically the National gambling industry focusing particularly at *on-line gaming*. With the authority granted to it by the *Gambling Act of 2005* the U.K.'s Gambling Commission ensures that gambling in the UK is crime-free, is fair and open and children and vulnerable people are protected from being harmed or exploited by gambling (Gambling Commission, UK, online, Gambling Act 2005).

The European Union Commission Recommendation of 14 July 2014, on principles for the protection of consumers and players of online gambling services and for the prevention of minors from gambling online (Text with EEA relevance - *2014/478/EU)* has not succeeded in providing a proper 'safety net' for EU citizens. In a relevant press release in December 2018, Maarten Haijer, Secretary General, EGBA noted:

"Because online gambling in Europe is regulated at national-level, the level of consumer protection provided to players varies depending on where they reside in the EU – and this is entirely inadequate for what is an inherently borderless digital sector. Guidelines have proven insufficient and we call on EU policymakers to act by introducing mandatory rules to ensure there is a consistent high-level of consumer protection and uniform safety nets for all online gamblers in Europe." (European Gaming & Betting Association, online, Press Release).

The EU Commission Recommendation mentioned above was reviewed in a study by EGBA which found that major gaps existed in consumer protection in E.U. member States (Carran, 2018).

It should be noted that the European Gaming and Betting Association (EGBA) is the Brussels-based industry body representing the leading online gaming and betting operators established, licensed and regulated within the EU. EGBA works together with National authorities, EU authorities and other stakeholders towards the achievement and maintenance of a well-regulated and attractive offer for EU citizens.

6 TYPOLOGY OF GAMBLERS AND GAMBLING

'The Gambler' (in Russian *Igrok*) was a short novel, characterized as a novella, authored by the Russian novelist Fyodor Dostoevsky (or Dostoyevsky, 1821-1881) which was published originally in Russian in 1866 and later translated into English in 1877. The novella served for many decades as a classic reference to the drama of compulsive gamblers and the destructive, financially, socially and emotionally gambling addiction. The novella's main character Aleksey Ivanovich, shows the typical evolution of the gambling disorder which usually unfolds in three well delineated phases: profits, losses and despair. Dostoyevsky, the author of the novella, ultimately managed to cure himself from his destructive gambling addiction.

In writing *'Dostoyevsky and Parricide'*, a focused paper analysing Dostoyevsky's other major work *'The brothers Karamazov'*, the father of psychoanalysis Dr Sigmund Freud suggested that compulsive gamblers, such as the Russian author who suffered from epileptic seizures, have an unconscious desire to lose, (the tendency is also described in other psychodynamic interpretive views as a form of 'masochism'). Such individuals gamble to relieve the feeling of guilt. In the specific paper Freud brought forth the eternal concept of 'Parricide' (the term describes the subconscious wish to kill one's father) present in some of the World's greatest works of literature such as *Oedipus Rex*, *Hamlet*, and *The Brothers Karamazov*. Freud in this papers related Dostoyevsky's subconscious parricidal feelings to his epilepsy (Jones, 1963).

If reading is one of your favourite pastimes then we would politely suggest to you, unless you have already done it, when your schedule will permit it, to read Dostoevsky's classic novella bearing the title *'The Gambler'*. Over and above the satisfaction of reading a great classic you will also discover some titillating details and fascinating trivia concerning the emotions he was experiencing and the reasons for which Dostoyevsky wrote the book in a very short time (Morson, 2020).

Dostoyevsky wrote a large part of his work while staying in Germany as is noted in a special section of **Deutschland.de** published 02.06.2014. While he was still engulfed in his pathological gambling condition he spent time in Wiesbaden, Bad Homburg and Baden-Baden being a regular visitor to the three German cities famed casinos. Indeed ever since each one of the three cities makes claim to the possibility that it was the *'Rouletteburg'* (the reference city he used in his novella *'The Gambler'*).

During the last few decades as a result of global attempts to assess typical individual profiles of gamblers an interesting typology has emerged which classifies them into three categories:

a. The *social gambler* category includes those individuals who gamble for entertainment, diversion or distraction and who can stop gambling whenever they want and decide to do so;
b. The *professional gambler* category includes those individuals who have made the life decision to select gambling as their means of earning a livelihood; and,
c. The *compulsive gambler* category includes those individuals, men women and youths, who gamble because their behavior is driven by their addiction to gambling and who are unable to stop their behavior (Halliday & Fuller, 1974; Custer, 1984; Dickerson & Adcock, 1987).

Attempts to identify the types of gambling prevalent in Europe, America, Canada, Australia and other industrially developed societies have isolated four predominant types of gambling:

a. *Gaming* or the exchange of money in a game in which chance plays a part (e.g. roulette),
b. *Betting* or the staking of money on a future event, or any event, the issue of which is doubtful or unknown to the participants in the wager (e.g. horse-racing gambling),
c. *Lotteries* or the distribution of a mutually contributed prize by lot (e.g. football pools), and
d. *Speculation,* which covers gambling activities conducted on any of the established exchange markets (e.g. commodity speculation) (Halliday & Fuller, op. cit., 1974; Custer, op.cit., 1984).

The spectrum of aetiological explanations concerning gambling behavior is indeed broad. However, two non-mutually exclusive types of motivation have been proposed: the desire for positively reinforcing subjective excitement and arousal; and the desire for the negatively reinforcing relief or escape from stress or negative emotional states. Both social and monetary reward expectancies facilitate gambling due to the learned association with, and capacity to enhance or regulate, positive affect (Shead & Hodgins, 2009).

At this point based on decades of research efforts and clinical experiences five major theoretical models on the aetiology of problem gambling have emerged which, in brief, are:

The Learning theory, according to which operant reinforcement and classical conditioning contingencies increase and maintain the individual's gambling behaviour.

The *Cognitive model*, which includes erroneous beliefs and distortions which motivate and drive the individual's gambling behaviour (e.g., the gambler's fallacy known also as the 'Monte Carlo fallacy' which in brief states that 'after a streak of losses here comes my win').

The *Addiction model*, which relates pathological gambling to 'substance' abuse, i.e. *'an addiction without the drugs'* since motivation and behaviour involves persistent urges, and participation, withdrawal and tolerance.

The *Personality theory* according to which identified patterns involve impulsive, sensation-seeking and risk-taking traits, and high rates of Axis II personality disorders, and finally,

The *Integrated models*, of multifactorial causation of problematic gambling behaviour bringing forth a combination of biopsychosocial variables subtyping their pathogenic origin.

Surely there is a plethora of research papers and theoretical treatises published in the last few decades which aim to understand and interpret individual gambling behaviour. As Australia is one of the outstanding countries where large numbers of individuals are involved in gambling, we call your attention to the final version of the Australian Psychological Society's review paper titled *'The Psychology of Gambling'* which was published in November, 2010 and is available as a 59 page PDF on line. As noted on page 15 of this publication *'no single or integrated model of gambling is able to explain the causal factors responsible for the development of pathological gambling. However, integrated models taking into account the multifactorial biopsychosocial variables appear to be gaining prominence'* (APS Gambling Working Group, online, pdf).

6.1   ROULETTES AND SLOT MACHINES

Gamblers, as well as individuals who gamble only occasionally, have access to a variety of machines known as *roulettes* in which they can 'try their luck'. Roulettes are available in special, brick and mortar, gambling establishments known as Casinos. The *'roulette'*, took its name from the French word meaning *'little wheel'*, and was invented in late 18th century in France. There are several urban-myths attempting to trace its creation from the French philosopher and mathematician Blaise Pascal to some less famous monastery monks and to Spanish merchants who introduced it to Europe. The roulette is mainly a casino game, but as we will discuss later in our digital age it is also encountered as an on-line casino game. In the roulette game, players may choose to place bets on either a single number, various groupings of numbers, the colors red or black, whether the number is odd or even, or if the numbers are high (19–36) or low (1–18).

The roulette table layout is usually the one where the roulette is located at the head of the table in front of the House-croupier. At the other end of the table the colored cloth, leather or plastic surface has all numbers, red or black color and even/odd demarcations and depending on the type of roulette the one zero (European style) or two zeros (American style) depicting respectively the two roulette types. It should be well emphasized here that when the ball falls into the one or the two zeroes the event translates into the reality that ALL bets are lost for the gamblers and the House is the winner.

Obviously, in terms of winning odds, the European one zero roulette type favors better the gamblers while the American two zero type favors the House. Gamblers stand (in some casinos chairs are provided for players to sit on) around the table and place their bets on the surface depicting the roulette. In some casinos there are two colored surfaces on the roulette table aiming at gathering more players around the roulette table as this will increase the volume of the House 'intake'. It should be added that several casinos around the globe provide the participating gamblers with small touch activated screens on which they can place their bets not having to do so on the colored roulette table surfaces. In many casinos curious by-standers who do not place bets are usually kindly invited to stand away from the roulette tables allowing more space for betting players.

While playing the game in order to determine the winning number and color, the process starts when the croupier spins the roulette wheel in one direction and then spins a ball in the opposite direction in a tilted circular track running around the outer edge of the wheel. The ball, following the rules of physics eventually loses momentum, passes through an area of deflectors, and falls onto the wheel and into one of 37 (single zero French/European style roulette) or 38 (double zero American style roulette) colored and numbered pockets on the wheel. The winnings are then paid to anyone who has placed a successful bet (Wikipedia, Roulette).

The roulette was used in the Royal Palace Paris Casino shortly before the end of the 18th century and then spread to other French casinos associated with Spas with immense success. Then competition emerged from a German casino located in the spa city of Bad Homburg vor der Höhe and operated by the Frenchman François Blanc (1806 - 1877). The competition to French casinos came from the innovation introduced by Blanc using a roulette with a single 0 slot (contrasting with the two 00 slots of French casino roulettes). The casino success with the new type of roulette in attracting wealthy as well as players representing Europe's nobility earned him the nickname '*Magician of Bad Homburg*'. According to the tourist city guide among Bad Homburg's casino internationally famous players was Fyodor Dostoyevsky (Bad Homburg, de. Brochure in English).

Credited with the immense success of the Bad Homburg casino in Germany, and facing the mid-19th century Frankfurt Assembly Laws negatively affecting the casino operations, Francois Blanc was given the privilege of managing gambling in Monaco through the intermediary of the *'Société des Bains de Mer et du Cercle des Etrangers'* (Monegasque tourism establishment which now owns gambling, entertainment and leisure properties). On the basis of the successful operation of the Monte Carlo casino, F. Blanc was nicknamed the *'Magician of Monte-Carlo'* (Principaute de Monaco, online, François Blanc).

Shortly before the end of the 19th century another type of gambling machine/instrument encountered in bars, restaurants and pubs as well as in gambling and betting high street shops, are the slot machines (known also as 'fruit machines' named after the variety of fruits shown on their screens and nicknamed *'one arm bandits'* as they had a large mechanical lever affixed to either side of the machine.). The person using the slot machine first drops a coin in the designated slot and then pulls the side handle getting the reels in motion. The slot machine is credited to a German immigrant Charles Augustus Fey, a mechanic living in San Francisco, California who constructed the first model in 1895.

There are, however, some myths relating to the fatherhood of the slot machine with some attributing the prototype to a Brooklyn, New York based Sittman and Pitt machine producing company who developed it in 1891. The Sittman and Pitt machine, a precursor to Fey's slot machine, contained five drums holding 50 cards used in a poker game. The user would drop his coin in the slot and pull the side lever waiting for the spin to show the desired 3 cards when it would come to a halt. In this machine there was no possibility of an immediate pay-off but the store owner would pass one to the user his win in kind (drinks, cigarettes, cigars, candies etc).

Charles Fey used only 3 spinning reels in his slot machine bearing images of spades, hearts, horseshoes, diamonds, and a Liberty Bell (from which the machine got the name 'Bell'). Fey's slot machine had the capacity to pay the user's win on the spot in nickels and dimes. Nowadays slot machines are operated electrically, have a variety of symbols, pictures and icons on their screens and spinning is enriched with musical themes and tones (Costa, 2013; Slots History, online; Bellis 2019 online).

7   THE PROFILE OF THE PATHOLOGICAL GAMBLER ACCORDING TO APA'S VARIOUS (DSMS)

Historically, behaviors, which have been associated with 'problem gambling' have been variously described as compulsive, addicted and pathological. Pathological gambling was first included as a diagnosable mental disorder in DSM-III in 1980 and it was defined as *'a chronic and progressive failure to resist impulses to gamble'* (Volberg & Steadman, 1988).

In 1980 the APA officially classifying pathological gambling as an impulse-control disorder placed it in a fuzzy label for a group of somewhat related illnesses that, at the time, included kleptomania, pyromania and trichotillomania (a tem referring to the compulsivity of hair pulling) (Jabr, 2013).

In the (DSM-III) the diagnostic criteria for pathological gambling were listed as follows:

a. The individual is chronically and progressively unable to resist impulses to gamble,
b. Gambling compromises, disrupts, or damages family, personal and vocational pursuits, as indicated by at least three of the following:

1. Arrest for forgery, fraud, embezzlement, or tax evasion due to attempts to obtain money for gambling,
2. default on debts or other financial responsibilities,
3. Disrupted family and/ or spouse relationship due to gambling,
4. Borrowing of money from illegal sources (e.g. loan sharks),
5. Inability to account for loss of money or to produce evidence of winning money, if this is claimed,
6. Loss of work due to absenteeism in order to pursue gambling activity,
7. Necessity for another person to provide money to relieve a desperate financial situation, and

c. The gambling is not due to antisocial personality disorder. Therefore, pathological gambling can be considered as a 'drugless' impulse disorder (Custer, 1984).

Compulsion is typically applied to a behavioral pattern characterized by the continual commitment of an irrational act that usually violates the individual's personal standards (Eadington, 1976). The compulsive gambler, by repute, is hooked on the act of gambling and will bet on anything given the opportunity to do so.

An interesting aspect of the different forms of gambling is the idea that compulsive gamblers may choose outlets that are more exciting with a high risk and more compulsive. Compulsive gambling is considered by some as an illness characterized by a variety of symptoms such as neglect of family, inefficiency at work, financial difficulties, marital difficulties, loss of control and general disturbances of economic, social and psychological functioning of the gambler and/ or the family as a result of persistent gambling (Orford, 1985; Volberg & Steadman, 1988).

Furthermore, debt, loss of employment and friends, eviction, loss of time at work or school, criminality, marital problems, family problems, depression, attempted suicide, irritability, restlessness, obsessional thoughts and behavior disorders in the children of compulsive gamblers might also occur (Moran, 1970; Walker, 1989; Glass, 1991).

As mentioned above *'pathological gambling'* was defined and included as an *'impulse disorder'* for the first time in the historic edition of the American Psychiatric Association's 'Diagnostic and Statistical Manual of Mental Disorders' (DSM-III) in 1980.

Much has been written in scientific literature, as well as in popular Mass Media articles and editorials, about the myths and realities and the *'whys and how's'* of the initial inclusion of *'pathological gambling'* in the historic (DSM-III) 1980 edition. Readers interested in learning more about the myths and realities of that decision can satiate their curiosity reading R.J. Rosenthal's article online titled 'Inclusion of pathological gambling in DSM-III, its classification as a disorder of impulse control, and the role of Robert Custer' (Rosenthal, 2019).

It is noteworthy that in the APA's next edition of the (DSM-IV) in 1994 *'pathological gambling'* was defined as persistent and recurrent maladaptive gambling behaviour. The pathological gambler was defined as a person whose behaviour included five (or more) of the list of the following 10 criteria:

1. is preoccupied with gambling (e.g., preoccupied with reliving past gambling experiences, handicapping or planning the next venture, or thinking of ways to get money with which to gamble)
2. needs to gamble with increasing amounts of money in order to achieve the desired excitement
3. has repeated unsuccessful efforts to control, cut back, or stop gambling

4. is restless or irritable when attempting to cut down or stop gambling
5. gambles as a way of escaping from problems or of relieving a dysphoric mood (e.g., feelings of helplessness, guilt, anxiety, depression)
6. after losing money gambling, often returns another day to get even ("chasing" one's losses)
7. lies to family members, therapist, or others to conceal the extent of involvement with gambling
8. has committed illegal acts such as forgery, fraud, theft, or embezzlement to finance gambling
9. has jeopardized or lost a significant relationship, job, or educational or career opportunity because of gambling
10. relies on others to provide money to relieve a desperate financial situation caused by gambling

In the current APA (DSM-V) edition published in 2013 *'pathological gambling'*, which was defined in (DSM-IV) as persistent and recurrent problematic gambling behaviour leading to clinically significant impairment or distress, was replaced in the (DSM-V) with the diagnosis of *'Gambling Disorder'*. This new definition applies and is indicated when the individual exhibits four (or more) of the new list of 9 criteria in a 12-month period. In (DSM-V) the criteria have been reduced to 9 since the criterion referring to the person who 'has committed illegal acts such as forgery, fraud, theft, or embezzlement to finance gambling' has been dropped.

8 THE CONCEPTION AND CREATION OF THE INTERNET AND THE WORLD WIDE WEB (WWW)

In this chapter of our book, we will discuss the modern condition of 'internet addiction'. We will proceed by taking a brief glimpse at the work of the two British scientists who are credited with the developments of the *'computer'* and the *'World Wide Web'*. Before doing that, however, we wish to bring to your attention a Smithsonian article on the so-called *'Antikythera mechanism'* (named after the place in our homeland Greece where it was discovered) which is currently located at the National Archaeological Museum in Athens which has been considered by some writers as 'the first computer' (Marchant, 2015).

In a Britannica article written by Michael R. Swaine and Paul A. Freiberger and titled *'Analytical Engine – Computer'* the two authors note that the 'Analytical Engine', designed and partly built in the 19th century by the British mathematician and inventor Charles Babbage as an improved version of his original creation the 'Difference Engine' (a calculating machine) does earn him the title of the conceptual pioneer-inventor of the modern calculating machines called computers (Swaine and Freiberger).

As Evan Andrews noted in his article in HISTORY (originally published on December 18, 2013 and revised on October 28, 2019) titled *'Who Invented the Internet?'* the internet cannot be credited to a single person as it is the result of the work of dozens of pioneering scientists, programmers and engineers. However, the first steps toward the internet as we know it today appeared in the early 1960's in the work of J. C. R. Licklider of the Massachusetts Institute of Technology (MIT) who popularized the idea of an 'Intergalactic Network' of computers. Andrews notes that the online world became more identifiable in 1990, when computer scientist Tim Berners-Lee invented the World Wide Web. While it's often confused with the internet itself, the web is actually just the most common means of accessing data online in the form of websites and hyperlinks (Andrews, 2019 October).

J. C. R. Licklider was a posthumous recipient of recognition by the Internet Hall of Fame in 2013 and on his page it is noted that: *'In 1962, Dr Joseph Carl Robnett Licklider formulated the earliest ideas of global networking in a series of memos discussing an "Intergalactic Computer Network." Both well-liked and well-respected, he demonstrated an amazing prescience many times over. His original and far-sighted ideas outlined many of the features the Internet offers today: graphical computing, user-friendly interfaces, digital libraries, e-commerce, online banking, and cloud computing'.* (Internet Hall of Fame, online).

Sir Tim Berners-Lee, a Briton computer scientist, is credited with the conception and creation in 1989 of the World Wide Web (WWW) while working at CERN, the globally renowned large particle physics laboratory located near Geneva, Switzerland. As noted in a 'History of the Web' article in The World Wide Web Foundation, already at that time, millions of computers were being connected together through the fast-developing **internet** and Berners-Lee realised they could share information by exploiting an emerging technology called hypertext. By October of 1990, Tim had written the three fundamental technologies that remain the foundation of today's web (and which you may have seen appear on parts of your web browser given below):

HTML: HyperText Markup Language. The Markup (formatting) language for the web.

URI: Uniform Resource Identifier. A kind of "address" that is unique and used to identify to each resource on the web. It is also commonly called a URL.

HTTP: Hypertext Transfer Protocol. Allows for the retrieval of linked resources from across the web.

Sir Tim moved from CERN to the Massachusetts Institute of Technology (MIT) in 1994 where he founded the World Wide Web Consortium (W3C), an international community devoted to developing open web standards. He remains there serving as the Director of W3C to this day (WWW Foundation, online).

Ever since he created the World Wide Web in 1989, which by now is used by half of the world's population, he has been hailed and cheered for his insistence that it should be made available FREE, which he succeeded doing!.. Sir Tim Berners-Lee was inducted on 27 July 2012 to the Internet Hall of Fame for his invention of the World Wide Web (WWW) (Internet Hall of Fame, online).

According to relevant data provided by the Internet World Stats in the summer of 2019, from an estimated 7.716,223,309 billion humans worldwide the internet users' population was 4,536,248,808. The specific statistics for both population and internet users in each of the major geopolitical regions of the Globe in mid-2019 given in alphabetical order were the following: Africa population 1,340,598,447 internet users 526,374,930; Asia population 4,294,516,659, internet users 2,300,469,859; *Europe* population 834,995.197, internet users 727,814,272; Latin America/Caribbean population 658,345,826, internet users 453,702,292; Middle East population 260,991,690, internet users 180,498,292; North America population 368,869,647, internet users 348,908,868; Oceania/Australia population 42,690,838, internet users 28,775,373 (Internet world statistics, 2019).

8.1 INTERNET ADDICTION: THE EMERGENCE OF A MODERN HUMAN CONDITION

We will make an attempt to describe with words a picture with which we choose to introduce you to the core matter of this sub-section of our book. Walking through the corridors of any modern shopping centre or 'Mall' in any large city across the European continent, Canada, USA and Latin America, or the Near East and the Far East including Australia and New Zealand you will see toddlers in their baby carriages pushed by mothers, fathers, grand parents or older siblings and you will see many of them holding in their hands a tablet, an IPad or their parents smartphone and absorbed in internet surfing or watching a You Tube video. You will also see kindergarten or early primary school children sitting at a coffee shop or restaurant table with their family absorbed in internet surfing or You Tube video watching on their electronic devices.

We can safely assume that you have witnessed such scenes during any of your visits to shopping Malls and perhaps on busy Main Streets in your own home towns. Nowadays, the road to internet surfing, which for some becomes an addictive behaviour, starts at a very early age...

Shortly before the end of the 20th century, in the middle of the 1990's, the numbers of online computer users were increasing at unprecedented rates and so were the vast amounts of attention and resources devoted toward the World-Wide Web. It was noted during the same time period that in a parallel manner social pathologies were beginning to surface in *cyberspace* and so did addictive behavior related to this new type of stimulation. At the end of the 20th century and before the entry to the third millennium and the first decade of the 21st century, it was estimated, by relevant research, that two to three per cent of the members of the on-line community were already exhibiting serious internet addiction behaviors. As the 20th century was coming to an end literally millions of individuals spent most of their waking time surfing, chatting in this medium, buying internet books, shopping, trading, trying out new WWW browsers, researching internet vendors or organizing files of downloaded material (Griffiths, 1999). Surveys were confirming that the stereotypes of computer-dependent people were mostly male, introverted, educated and likely to use computers in their profession (Pitkow & Kehoe, 1996).

Excessive use of the Internet, as Griffiths has noted a couple of decades ago, features some core components of addiction namely, salience, mood modification, tolerance, withdrawal, conflict and relapse which will be briefly presented below (Griffiths, 1996; 1999).

Salience occurs when the Internet becomes the most important activity in the person's life as it dominates thinking (leading to preoccupations and cognitive distortions), feelings (resulting in craving) and behavior (socialized behavior deteriorates, or important social, occupational or recreational activities are given up, reduced or affected).

Mood modification relates to the subjective experiences that people report as a consequence of engaging in Internet usage and can be seen as a coping strategy. People can be tempted by this second online life (chat rooms), that is completely a fantasy life, of people that they have never met but they feel more emotionally connected to than people in their real lives. Stay-at-home mothers are particularly prone, as are certain personality types, such as the very shy individuals.

Tolerance is the process whereby increasing amounts of Internet use are required to achieve the same effects. Furthermore, withdrawal symptoms are the unpleasant feelings or physical effects that occur when Internet usage is discontinued or suddenly reduced such as, psychomotor agitation, anxiety, obsessive thinking about what is happening on Internet, fantasies or dreams about Internet and voluntary or involuntary typing movements of the fingers.

Conflict refers to the conflicts involving Internet use between addicts and those around them (interpersonal conflict, marital difficulties, feelings of abandonment in significant others), conflicts with other activities (job, social life, hobbies and interests) or from within individuals themselves (intrapsychic conflict). For example, dozens of divorce cases are reported to have emerged in which one spouse charged the other with excessive online activities at the expense of the marriage and the children. Furthermore, with the promotion of the Internet people abuse it to the detriment of some aspect of their real life, whether it is marriage, their jobs or their schools.

Finally, *relapse* is the tendency for reversions to earlier patterns of Internet use to recur, and for even the most extreme patterns typical of the height of the addiction to be quickly restored after many years of abstinence or control (Griffiths, 2000; 2005).

Internet addiction can manifest itself with the need to log on daily and become so absorbed in the activity that the users forget almost everything else in their real daily lives. Typical signs of online addiction are: losing track of time once online; minimizing to others the amount of time spent online; anticipation of online usage; others complain about the amount of time spent online; others complain about a large phone bill related to time spent online; daily home use of online services; high phone bills related to online service fees and connect time; logged on to personal account while at work; poor interpersonal relationships due to increased time spent online; and sneaking online when their *significant other* is not at home.

The late Dr. Kimberly Young (who founded the Center for Internet Addiction in 1995) was the creator of the 'Internet Addiction Diagnostic Questionnaire' (IADQ) which consists of 8 criteria, it is provided on line in the CIA site, and according to its creator meeting 5 of the following criteria means you are addicted: (1) Do you feel preoccupied with the Internet (think about previous online activity or anticipate next online session)? (2) Do you feel the need to use the Internet with increasing amounts of time in order to achieve satisfaction? (3) Have you repeatedly made unsuccessful efforts to control, cut back, or stop Internet use? (4) Do you feel restless, moody, depressed, or irritable when attempting to cut down or stop Internet use? (5) Do you stay online longer than originally intended? (6) Have you jeopardized or risked the loss of significant relationship, job, educational or career opportunity because of the Internet? (7) Have you lied to family members, therapist, or others to conceal the extent of involvement with the Internet? And (8) Do you use the Internet as a way of escaping from problems or of relieving a dysphoric mood (e.g., feelings of helplessness, guilt, anxiety, depression) (Young, 1998).

9 THE INTERNET AS A VEHICLE FOR INDIVIDUALS' ONLINE TRADING

Starting toward the end of the 20th century and continuing into the 21st century, increasing numbers of individuals in America, Europe and other industrial, economically developed countries are becoming online traders.

Using the term *'trading nation'* CNBC makes a great case for the democratization of the stock market as people have entered the Age of the Individual Investor. People are reported to talk about the stock market now in the same way they talk about their health or their kids' schools or the weather. As a relevant CNBC on-line comment has noted: *'Trading Nation is a multimedia financial news program that shows investors and traders how to use the news of the day to their advantage. This is where experts from across the financial world – including macro strategists, technical analysts, stock-pickers, and traders who specialize in options, currencies, and fixed income – come together to find the best ways to capitalize on recent developments in the market. Trading Nation: Where headlines become opportunities'* (CNBC- trading NATION).

Today not only those who live in America but all English speaking individual traders across the Globe can have access to a continuous 24 hour flow of information by tuning into the major TV channels such as the American CNBC, CNN-Business, Bloomberg business TV which reaches over 300 million homes globally, as well as the British BBC's business programs, and Germany's DW Business programs, France's BFM business channel covering Worldwide economic news. At this point, purely for historical reasons, we should mention CNNfn which was an American cable television news network operated by the CNN subsidiary of the media conglomerate Time Warner from November 29, 1995, and of AOL Time Warner until December 15, 2004 when it ceased to exist and its programs went off-the-air.

People who have become online traders have their portfolios constantly updated on their office computers (this practice has lead numerous national and international corporations to prohibit their employees to upload personal stuff on their office computers). Online traders know which of their neighbors like mutual funds and which neighbors trade Internet stocks. Half the population, according to Nocera, has become an investment club. There is a level of awareness and a level of sophistication about the market that is simply unprecedented. It has become part of the popular culture. It is one of the great cultural transformations of today (Nocera & Chen, October 11, 1999).

The attraction of the online trading is obvious. With a click of a mouse, through any one of scores of online brokers, people can buy and sell any stock, bond, forex contract or even crypto currencies anywhere in the world, day or night, cutting transaction costs by two thirds or more. Furthermore, there are online banks, online mortgage brokers, online business news services, and investing chat rooms for cyber squabbling over stocks. In fact, as we mentioned above at the beginning paragraphs of this section of our book, an entire parallel e-universe of financial services had opened for business at the end of the 20th century and has immensely expanded during the first two decades of the 21st century. As we mentioned above, today online traders have continuous financial information flow from globally transmitting channels – CNBC, CNN-business and Bloomberg, as well as Internet sites such as Yahoo, thus being able to acquire all the relevant stock information they need in order to engage in their daily online trading activity.

Finding the exact number of individuals engaging in online stock trading on a global scale is an elusive target, more than simply difficult to achieve and present with a proper sense of scientific reliability and objectivity. Determining the number of individual investors who fall into the category of 'addicted' online traders is surely and simply a contemporary Herculean task.

Bringing to our readers material relating to these internet/stock market realities we have used two reports. The first report was published in FORTUNE magazine in 1999, just before the end of the 20th century, was authored by Andy Serwer and his associates Christine Y. Chen, Angela Key and was uploaded in CNN-Money. Andy Serwer's, C. Y. Chen's and A. Key's FORTUNE, 11 October 1999 article was uploaded in CNN Money with the title: *'There is a revolution under way, and it is changing the way people invest in the stock market, work and live. Money is no longer with some broker or fund manager, but money is with people themselves.'* According to the authors Investing has become part of everyday life and America had become the land of the 'self–invested' through online brokerage. The authors' response to the question how big is online trading, was that some 42 million out of 99 million American households have PCs, and 24 million have Internet access. About 12 million of those households now have online accounts, and those folks are making more than a half-million trades a day. The percentage of U.S. investors trading online is now about 12.5% and is expected to climb to 29.2% by 2002 (Serwer, et al 1999).

Relevant statistics indicate that among adults 74% of Americans owned a desktop or laptop computer while in the UK 88% of households owned a home computer in 2018 (Statista US 2020; Statista UK 2020).

Brokernotes 2018 Report is titled '*The Modern Trader – Traders aren't who they used to be*'. According to the Report 1 out of every 634 people on this planet trade on line and the total number of traders is now 13.9 million worldwide and of them 2.7 million are female traders. Using residence in a Continent or a Region as the geopolitical characteristic for the identification of the online traders the statistical results are as follows: Asia, (4,600,000), Europe (3,100,000), Africa (2,000,000), North America (1,600,000), Middle East (980,000), South America (760,000), Central America (450,000) and Oceania (410,000). Looking at the numbers of online traders in Europe we see the United Kingdom is in top with 730,000 Germany (380,000), France (280,000), Italy (260,000), Spain (200,000), and Netherlands (190,000) (Brokernotes 2018).

Two possible views have emerged in the effort to explain why online trading is expanding. The first is the investor-empowerment theory, which says that the Internet is a positive thing for investors. It pushes the securities industry to offer after-hours trading and to create new exchanges. Furthermore, it forces direct distribution of IPOs (initial price offerings), the opening up of conference calls. Finally, it expands investor-relation functions at companies. The second, on the other hand, is the investor-excitability theory, which says that the Internet just makes investors excited. It is a fact that the online experience increases trading. Clearly, that is good for brokers, but is not always so for investors.

However, with online trading becoming an easy way to get in on the high-stakes world of stocks, bond, currency and other financial markets, many people do not realize that it can be as addictive as gambling. The problem can easily become even more serious for '*day-traders*' as they stand to lose far more money than casino gamblers. Generally, the profile of the average day trader mirrors that of a compulsive gambler as they both tend to be young males in their 20s or 30s who look at stock market trading as a scheme to get rich quick. Online trading is a huge casino for many people. Thus, day trading can be no different from other forms of gambling. The criteria to determine whether someone has a gambling problem with the stock market involve the nature of their activity in the market and their state of mind (Piperopoulou, 2004; 2010).

When the stock market takes a 'nosedive', so potentially can the mental health of online traders. People see how their money is being lost, and their emotions run higher. Trading from the desktop, via the Internet, is surely cheaper and more convenient than going through a broker or financial planner. But often the price of that convenience is stress. People are turning themselves into a trader, a profession notorious for high anxiety. The ability to make rapid decisions within a few seconds to a couple of minutes is the hallmark of online stock market trading (Joslyn & Hunt, 1998).

Furthermore, on top of the stress of bringing the Wall Street trading floor to one's desk, there is also the loneliness factor. When the markets decline there is no one there to comfort the online trader since humanity does not exist online. And if things do not go well, in the case of online traders the only one to blame is oneself. In their article titled: '*Is Pathological Trading an Overlooked Form of Addiction?*' Guglielmo, Ioime and Janiri after noting that the mental health community seems to have taken lightly the phenomenon of a 'trading addiction.' They boldly express their belief that the presence of pathological trading among investors is a real phenomenon and that also represents an important public health problem that deserves the attention of the scientific community. They note that pathological trading leads to a progressive loss of control over trading, tolerance and withdrawal symptoms similar to the symptoms present in substance use disorders (Guglielmo et al., 2016).

10 THERAPEUTIC TREATMENT OF PATHOLOGICAL GAMBLERS: '12-STEP' FELLOWSHIP, CBT & DRUGS

'*Disordered gambling*', as a behavioral addiction is the currently used term in APA's (DSM-V) referring to the classic *pathological gambling* term which for many decades was viewed as a phenomenon falling within the causal boundaries of the Obsessive-Compulsive Disorders (OCD) and individuals were treated with appropriate to OCD drugs. In a review paper examining a large number of empirical studies on adult gambling in the time period since the year 2,000 the reported worldwide rates ranging from (0.12-5.8%) signify that pathological gambling is a serious matter calling for serious global public health concerns (Calado and Griffiths, 2016).

It is not an exaggeration to state that so far the treatment of pathological gamblers, as reported in scientific research findings and Mass Media news stories and editorials, falls within the general boundaries of treatment approaches and methods used in dealing with other types of addictions such as dependencies on alcohol and substances. The main approaches include the mutual support, 12-step fellowship '*Gamblers Anonymous*' (GA) borrowing its name and its general philosophy, approach and modus operandi from AA which we already discussed in Part One; Cognitive Behavioral Therapy (CBT), and medically prescribed and administered drugs which aim to deal therapeutically and help underlying psychological-mental health problems.

10.1 GAMBLERS ANONYMOUS (GA)

In line with the implications of the above statement we will start with a brief reference to the GA (Gamblers Anonymous) 12-step fellowship program tailored after the original fellow support program of AA (Alcoholic Anonymous).

The fellowship of GA was founded by Jim W. in 1957 in Los Angeles, USA. He was a drinker and a gambler. He had joined Alcoholics Anonymous (AA) in 1946 and, seeing its benefits, applied similar principles to help himself with his gambling addiction. GA does not solicit members, there are no fees involved, and it is non-sectarian, without political or religious affiliations (Cambridge core, 2013).

The GA founding father, Jim W. (born as Jim Willis) died of heart failure on Nov. 22, 1983 aged 80. He founded the organization with the help of columnist Paul Coates, of the Los Angeles Mirror. Coates was well known for his popular daily newspaper column and also as the host of the syndicated tabloid-style television series *Confidential File*. There were 13 people at the first GA meeting (UPI, December 7, 1983).

In May, 1964, a member of Gamblers Anonymous, on business from the USA in England, attended a meeting addressed by the Secretary of the Churches Council of Gambling. The two men accepted that they must work together to establish the movement in Britain and a GA group was formed in London on 10th July, 1964 (GA, UK our history).

Today the fellowship of Gamblers Anonymous, according to information provided by the organization on line, has groups operating in over 56 countries across the Globe. Along with the regular GA meetings in many chapters across the Globe parallel meetings under the title of Gam-Anon are held for family members of gamblers who are participating in the 12-step fellowship meetings (Gamblers anonymous, Gam-Anon).

The 12-steps of the Gamblers Anonymous fellowship suggested as 'a program for recovery' having substituted the term *alcohol* with the term *gambling* to the original 12-step Alcoholics Anonymous list are the following:

1. We admitted we were powerless over gambling - that our lives had become unmanageable.
2. Came to believe that a Power greater than ourselves could restore us to a normal way of thinking and living.
3. Made a decision to turn our will and our lives over to the care of this Power of our own understanding.
4. Made a searching and fearless moral and financial inventory of ourselves.
5. Admitted to ourselves and to another human being the exact nature of our wrongs.
6. Were entirely ready to have these defects of character removed.
7. Humbly asked God (of our understanding) to remove our shortcomings.
8. Made a list of all persons we had harmed and became willing to make amends to them all.
9. Make direct amends to such people wherever possible, except when to do so would injure them or others.
10. Continued to take personal inventory and when we were wrong, promptly admitted it.

11. Sought through prayer and meditation to improve our conscious contact with God as we understood Him, praying only for knowledge of His will for us and the power to carry that out.

12. Having made an effort to practice these principles in all our affairs, we tried to carry this message to other compulsive gamblers (GA Recovery programme-the twelve steps of recovery).

The nature of anonymity characterizing the Gamblers Anonymous as we already pointed out in our relevant discussion of Alcoholic Anonymous presents serious problems in reaching reliable statistical results of success rates in dealing with the problematic-pathological gamblers. In earlier evaluations, Stewart and Brown (1998) concluded that GA alone does not appear to be sufficient to produce recovery for the majority of problem gamblers. Subsequent studies have employed comparative designs to evaluate the efficacy of GA oriented treatment programs, demonstrating equivalent results (Toneatto & Dragonetti, 2008). Other studies have suggested that a combination of regular participation in a Gamblers Anonymous group and in undergoing several Cognitive Behavioral Therapy (CBT) sessions with a qualified therapist was more successful in helping the gamblers than sole participation in GA sessions (Petry et al. 2006).

10.2 PSYCHOTHERAPEUTIC TREATMENT OF PATHOLOGICAL GAMBLERS

Pathological gambling is a complex psychosocial disorder with potential, as is the case with individuals with alcohol and drugs disorders of biological, (heredity related) underpinnings. Modern societies' liberal approach to gambling behavior combined on a global scale with elusive and unclear legislation governing the advertisement and ease of use of various games and bet placings (especially online) appear to exacerbate the individuals' path toward pathological gambling behavior.

Behavior and counselling therapies in their variety of forms as adapted by practitioners and especially Cognitive Behavioral Therapy (CBT) appear to be the most promising type in dealing with the cases of pathological gamblers. In general terms, CBT uses systematic exposure to the behavior gamblers should unlearn and teaches them specific skills to control and reduce their gambling urges. Cognitive Behavioral Therapy, as we already have outlined when discussing the treatment of alcoholics, focuses on identifying unhealthy, irrational and negative beliefs held by the individual and replacing them with healthy, positive ones. Enlisting the help and support of the gamblers' families it is not unusual to have the gambler and family members engage in some form of Family therapy running parallel with individual therapy provided to the gambler.

Cooperating with their therapists and family members pathological gamblers are able to point out *'critical incidents'* which relate to reinforcing their gambling behaviour such as available on pay-day cash, or passing by a brick and mortar casino establishment of their city. Behavioural management techniques used in the treatment of pathological gamblers include limiting access to money and/or applying a variety of techniques to increase the degree of difficulty to gamble. Casino gamblers in many countries are eligible to sign up for *a self-exclusion ban* from the casinos. However, both co-authors have had personal experiences with friends who had signed 'self-exclusions' from all Greek casinos BUT with the availability of online playing and with a plethora of online casinos at the Internet, gamblers kept engaging in their gambling and losing money. Disconnecting the Internet on their house PC does not restrict the gambler and makes no real difference as gambling is globally available with special apps on smartphones.

10.3 PHARMACOTHERAPY AS THE DRUG USING TREATMENT APPROACH

In the last few decades pathological gamblers (PG) have been pharmacologically treated with a variety of drugs and a broad variation of results have been recorded. It should be noted here that in this respect antidepressants, mood stabilizers and atypical antipsychotics have shown mixed results in controlled clinical trials. Although limited information is available, opioid antagonists and glutamatergic agents have demonstrated efficacious outcomes, especially for individuals with PG suffering from intense urges to engage in the behaviour (Grant et al., 2014).

Pathological gambling was classified in the American Psychiatric Association's (APA) Diagnostic Statistical Manual (DSM-III) of 1980 and again in the (DSM-IV) of 1994 as *'an impulse-control disorder not classified elsewhere' as indicated by the presence of 5 or more of a list of 10 specific criteria.* In the 2013 edition (DSM-V), the so-called *gambling disorder* was removed from the "Impulse Control Disorder" section and added to the newly expanded "Substance-related and Addictive Disorders" section.

With this move, *gambling disorder* has become the first recognized nonsubstance behavioral addiction, implying many shared features between gambling disorder and substance use disorders and, consequently, necessitating changes in the pharmacological and psychological treatment of individual gamblers. Stated in simple terms, under this new viewpoint concerning the treatment of individuals exhibiting *gambling disorder*, potentially innovative combinations of pharmacotherapy and psychotherapy could prove to yield better outcomes than the single use of either treatment approach (Huhn et al., 2014). Currently, opioid antagonists are considered the first-line treatments to reduce symptoms of uncontrolled gambling. Only recently, glutamatergic agents and combined pharmacological and psychological treatments have been examined appearing promising options for the management of the gambling disorder (Goslar et al. 2019).

PART THREE - SUBSTANCES

11 DRUG ADDICTION – AN INTRIGUING SPECTRUM OF RESPONSES WHEN ASKING 'WHY DRUGS?'

Anastasia-Natasha worked with persons suffering from substance use disorder over two decades ago after having received her BSc and MSc degrees in Health Psychology from the British University of Surrey. Following her graduation and return to her homeland she volunteered her services as a trainee in the drug addict therapeutic rehabilitation program (18+) of the Attica Psychiatric Hospital of Greece. Her duties included initial client intake and profile evaluation with the use of the "EuropASI" questionnaire, running individual and group therapeutic sessions, overseeing the clients' re-entry to the community processes and analysis of epidemiological research data. She had already been familiar with the world of addicts and the realities of addiction hearing her father, co-author of this book, in his many public speeches, TV and Radio presentations and Press articles who has had several decades of experience dealing with addicts at both sides of the Atlantic.

Georgios had his first contact with addicts while he was a senior honours student at the City College of the City University of New York. He had been invited along with a handful of classmates by his Psychology Professor, the late Dr Kenneth B. Clark, to visit Harlem and have first-hand experiences of Dr Clark's Harlem Youth Opportunities Unlimited (HARYOU) project.

At a Harlem Youth Centre for drug users Georgios met 'Jimmy' a 15 year old negro teenager (in the 1960's the term was 'negro', it changed later to 'black' and also to 'Afro-American') who was shooting dope (heroin). When, after a few meetings, Georgios naively asked "Jimmy' "Why drugs?" he received an answer which stayed with Georgios for several years; 'I am shooting dope for over a year now', Jimmy said, 'having started with marijuana when I was 11...You see when you are a teenager living in Harlem in a broken-up family with two more brothers from 2 different fathers but sharing the same mother, when you don't know if you will be attacked as you step out of your apartment building door and you know you don't have any future prospects, then you smoke grass and you shoot dope to escape from this miserable reality...Having 'no place in the sun' you use drugs fooling yourself that you found a 'place in the sun' you dreamt of..."

Georgios as an undergraduate foreign student working towards his honours degree in sociology and psychology summarized in his mind an aetiological hypothesis concluding that 'disadvantaged youth, from discriminated ethnic minorities will be prone to use drugs engaging in vain attempts to escape their miserable, unbearable, dramatic daily realities'.

For the next few years while working as a junior academic staff member Georgios was also active as a consultant to several drug-addict rehabilitation programs in the New England States of Rhode Island and Massachusetts. While serving as consultant to a 'Therapeutic Community' program in Massachusetts he met 'Jill' a 16 year old white female teenager 'user' brought to the 'T.C.' by the program's 'outreach team'. The members of the program's outreach team composed of ex-addicts and current residents undergoing rehabilitation, had met 'Jill' at the famous Harvard Square while she was begging by-passers for money she needed for her next 'dope shot'. Obtaining the consent of her family the young heroin user named 'Jill' was required to be subjected to the TC's 'intake interview'.

During the interview it became clear that 'Jill' was not a disadvantaged adolescent coming from a poor Boston neighbourhood having no 'place in the sun'. She belonged to an upper middle class family. She was enrolled in a private secondary Boarding school and she could easily get 'any place in the sun' she wished. Despite his lengthy experiences, Georgios posed to her, in his perennial 'naïve' style the question he had placed a few years ago to 'Jimmy' in Harlem: "Why drugs?"

The answer 'Jill' gave to Georgios during the 'intake interview' fully shattered to pieces the assumptions he had made when 'Jimmy' had given him when he was asked "Why drugs?".

'Why not?' Jill said as she, with an admirable eloquence for a teenager, went on to add:

'When you are born rich, you have always had almost everything you wanted and everything you asked for, when your parents provided artefacts money could buy but not enough and true love, when they send you to an expensive Boarding School you will try drugs, a prohibited venue, seeking to escape from what you experience as meaningless, loveless, boring daily realities...'

Georgios as a social-behavioural post graduate student was familiar with the then prevalent general causal framework describing an individual's transformation from an occasional user of substances to a pathological substance use disorder person. The relevant causal framework for this type of transformation included such factors as potential biological propensity; living in and growing up in a problematic family; succumbing to peer pressures to frequent participation in 'fun producing rave parties using substances'. Additional causal factors related to underlying mental health problems, including neurotic tendencies such as compulsion and anxiety.

Trying to reconcile in his mind the two diametrically opposite responses he had received and from Harlem's Jimmy and Boston's Jill, Georgios started then and has never stopped since, toying with the assumption that the spectrum of potential responses anyone could get posing the simple question "Why drugs?" is almost as broad, as the number of persons enmeshed in the inhumane condition of being an addict.

Certainly scientists, parents, Governmental Health and Law enforcement agencies and all others concerned use and rely on the multi-factor causal models in understanding and dealing with the problems of drug addiction, of substance use disorder; albeit each individual addict lives and experiences as a purely personal condition daily his or her dramatic reality.

Closing this personal account we inform our readers that during the Sixties and Seventies Georgios served in a variety of positions in the field of services provided to drug users acting as consultant and as a high ranking, executive level staff member in Therapeutic Communities. Indeed, during those early stages of 'Concept' T.C.'s he was one of a very small number of professionals in T.C.'s where the vast majority of staff were paraprofessional 'ex-addicts'.

12 SUBSTANCE USE DISORDER (SUD): A GLOBAL REALITY WITH ITS OWN SPECIAL VOCABULARY

We will open our discussion on substance use disorder in a somewhat unorthodox manner noting that anything in life is capable of becoming an addiction (Marks, 1990). Addictions have been many and varied throughout the history of mankind. Modern societies, characterized by a multitude of dependencies and inter-dependencies of men, machines and technological innovations, appear to create a vast reservoir of potentially threatening and hitherto unknown to man possibilities of developing addictive patterns of behavior. Thus, addictions have become a crucial problem that afflicts millions of individuals and disrupts the lives of their families, friends and associates (McMorran, 1994).

Continuing in this unorthodox manner in opening our discussion on SUD, we will bring to your attention an informative, enlightening and very useful US Drug Enforcement Administration (DEA) 'unclassified' document serving as a dictionary of slang terms for drugs (which are listed in alphabetical order) provided by the Drug Enforcement Administration's Houston, Texas Division, which was published in July, 2018 as an updated version to the product entitled "Drug Slang Code Words" originally published by the DEA in May 2017.

This new DEA document is available on line and titled: 'Slang Terms and Code Words: A Reference for Law Enforcement Personnel'. In our book we are using this valuable Report considering it not only useful and richly informative for Police personnel but also for much broader audiences which include teachers, academics, researchers, and surely students who are registered for University addiction modules at both the undergraduate and post-graduate levels as well as members of the general public interested in the subject of addictions as well as parents (DEA Intelligence report, July 2018).

At the eastern shores of the Atlantic, the European Monitoring Centre for Drugs and Drug Addiction (EMCDDA) is the central source and confirmed authority on drug-related issues in Europe. Based in Lisbon, the EMCDDA is one of the decentralised agencies of the European Union. European Monitoring Centre for Drugs and Drug Addiction (EMCDDA), European Drug Report 2019: Trends and Developments, Publications Office of the E.U., Lisbon, provides summaries on national drug phenomena in 30 countries and is available in 24 languages in pdf form (EMCDDA 2019).

Across the Globe daily, weekly, monthly, yearly drug addiction and drug overdose claim countless lives. The sad irony is that the deaths of dozens of thousands of ordinary people are not covered in newspaper front pages or on radio and television news programs. However, when celebrities die due to overdose or long term dependencies and addiction to substances their death 'makes the news'.

In this respect we call your attention to an article in 'USA Today' published June 3, 2016 as the Midwest Medical Examiner's office disclosing that the musician Prince, aged 57 died from an accidental fentanyl overdose. The USA Today article and an online article of the American 'drugs.com' service provide lists of celebrities who died as a result of substance addiction including, among others, in alphabetical order and age at death in parenthesis: John Belushi (33), Peaches Geldof (25), Jose Fernandez (24), Jimi Hendrix (27), Whitney Houston (48), Michael Jackson (50), Janis Joplin (27), Lil Peep (21), Marilyn Monroe (36), River Phoenix (23), Elvis Presley (42), and Amy Winehouse (27) (USA Today 2016).

In this respect interested readers can visit the online Drugs.com site based in the USA which provides along useful information names of notable celebrities and athletes who have had drugs or alcohol implicated in their deaths (Drugs.com online, Retrieved February 14, 2020).

Later on in this section of our book, we will make brief references to another, contemporary historically tragic irony. This one relates to the discovery of new drugs, initially very broadly prescribed to be used for therapeutic reasons and then, abruptly, imposing prohibition of their use when it was discovered that they turned out to create dependency, being addictive. We will present our readers with several cases of drugs which, from the 19th century to our times, when originally invented and sold were considered helpful in treating a variety of human health problems and widely dispersed without any control. Several drugs falling into this category eventually were detected as being harmful and placed under a variety of Governmental controls, to be used under careful medical supervision carrying heavy financial and penal punishments for illegal, unauthorized use.

12.1 THE AMERICAN GOVERNMENT'S REPETITIOUS DECLARATION OF 'WAR ON DRUGS'

At this point we bring to your attention the U.S. Federal Government's efforts to combat the use of narcotic substances deemed catastrophic for individuals and families and creating heavy burdens to Public Health facilities both in financial and treatment services. America, starting especially at the second half of the 19th century at the aftermath of the Civil War when countless uniformed men and non-uniformed civilians became addicted to morphine initially dispensed as a pain killer, and subsequently at the onset of the 20th century, engaged in 'a war against drugs'.

On January 23, 1912 the Hague International Opium Convention was ratified and signed thus establishing the groundwork for the evolving international system of drug control with the contracting powers committing themselves to restrict the use of drugs listed in the Convention to medical and other legitimate purposes. The drugs named in the 'protocol' were opium, morphine, heroin and cocaine. Original signatories to the Treaty which concluded the International Opium Conference held at The Hague from December 1, 1911, to January 23, 1912 were The United States, China, France, Germany, Great Britain, Italy, Japan, The Netherlands, Portugal, Russia, Siam, and Persia (US Dept. of State, Office of the Historian 2012).

Following the 1912 Hague Convention and the controls to be exercised in the traffic of opium, morphine, heroin and cocaine, in December 1914 the US Federal Government voted the Harrison Anti-Narcotics Tax Act (taking the name of its sponsor Representative Francis Burton Harrison of New York). The Harrison Act aimed to regulate and tax production, importation, and distribution of opiates and coca products. It stipulated that physicians and pharmacists dispensing them should keep careful and detailed records of the prescriptions written and executed.

In the late 1960's as a massive withdrawal of American troops from the Vietnam battlegrounds was unfolding and they were repatriated, countless numbers were identified as heroin users presenting a serious epidemic level reality. In March 1971 during a White House event and later on in July of 1971 addressing the US Congress President Richard Nixon declared a 'War on Drugs' (some suggest in mimicking President Lyndon Johnson's declaration on 'War on Poverty'). President Nixon proclaimed *"America's public enemy number one in the United States is drug abuse. In order to fight and defeat this enemy, it is necessary to wage a new, all-out offensive..."* (Sharp 1994).

Two years later in July, 1973 President Nixon created the Federal Government's Drug Enforcement Administration (DEA) which combined two already existing Federal Agencies, namely the Bureau of Narcotics and Dangerous Drugs (BNDD) and the Office of Drug Abuse Law Enforcement (ODALE) as well as some other smaller entities engaging in drug control. The DEA was staffed by employees of these two Agencies and several hundred other special agents and was mandated to enforce domestically and abroad the Federal Government's drug laws and carry through relevant drug control activities (DEA History).

Several important events took place in the USA during 1972. The Food and Drug Administration (FDA) approved the use of methadone for treating heroin addiction while during the same year the 'Drug Abuse Treatment Act of 1972' created the Special Action Office for Drug Abuse Prevention which laid the groundwork for the creation in 1974 of the National Institute on Drug Abuse (NIDA). Finally, TASC (Treatment Alternatives to

Street Crime) was also introduced by the Drug Abuse and Treatment Act to screen addicts in the Criminal Justice System and then to link and manage their involvement in treatment services. As a matter of fact many Therapeutic Communities across the Nation admitted addicts ordered to undergo treatment by 'Court referrals'. In 1987 while the American Medical Association declared that all drug dependencies should be considered as legitimate medical conditions and encouraged their treatment by physicians, President Ronald Reagan formally announced a renewed 'War on Drugs'. Statistics on the effect of the renewed 'War on Drugs' point to a lessened emphasis on treatment and increased emphasis toward punishment and incarceration (White, 1998).

13 CURRENT VIEW OF SUBSTANCE ABUSE & DEPENDENCE AS 'SUBSTANCE USE DISORDER' (SUD)

Under the title: *'The Science of Drug Use and Addiction: The Basics'* A National Institute on Drug Abuse (NIDA) paper available on line (last revised in July 2018), notes that 'The American Psychiatric Association's *'Diagnostic and Statistical Manual of Mental Disorders'*, (DSM-5) published in 2013 has replaced the categories of *substance abuse* and *substance dependence* with a single category: *substance use disorder, (SUD)* and introduced (as it did with alcohol) three sub-classifications—*mild, moderate, and severe.* The symptoms associated with a substance use disorder (SUD) fall into four major groupings: *impaired control, social impairment, risky use, and pharmacological criteria (i.e., tolerance and withdrawal).*

In this NIDA paper it is noted that DSM-5 provides 10 or 11 specific criteria (depending on the substance used) noting that an individual who in the preceding 12 month period meets two or three criteria is considered to have a *'mild'* disorder, when the individual meets four or five is considered to have a *'moderate'* disorder while an individual who meets six or more symptoms, is considered to have a *'severe'* disorder. The DSM-V diagnostic criteria are the following:

1. The substance is often taken in larger amounts or over a longer period than was intended.
2. There is a persistent desire or unsuccessful effort to cut down or control use of the substance.
3. A great deal of time is spent in activities necessary to obtain the substance, use the substance, or recover from its effects.
4. Craving, or a strong desire or urge to use the substance, occurs.
5. Recurrent use of the substance results in a failure to fulfil major role obligations at work, school, or home.
6. Use of the substance continues despite having persistent or recurrent social or interpersonal problems caused or exacerbated by the effects of its use.
7. Important social, occupational, or recreational activities are given up or reduced because of use of the substance.
8. Use of the substance is recurrent in situations in which it is physically hazardous.

9. Use of the substance is continued despite knowledge of having a persistent or recurrent physical or psychological problem that is likely to have been caused or exacerbated by the substance.
10. Tolerance, as defined by either of the following:
    a. A need for markedly increased amounts of the substance to achieve intoxication or desired effect.
    b. A markedly diminished effect with continued use of the same amount of the substance.
11. Withdrawal, as manifested by either of the following:
    a. The characteristic withdrawal syndrome for that substance (as specified in the DSM-5 for each substance).
    b. The use of a substance (or a closely related substance) to relieve or avoid withdrawal symptoms.

The relevant (NIDA) paper mentioned above highlights also the National Institute on Drug Abuse use of the terms *drug use, misuse,* and *addiction* and as we feel that this is an interesting as well as a useful differentiation we quote directly:

*"**Drug use** refers to any scope of use of illegal drugs: heroin use, cocaine use, tobacco use. **Drug misuse** is used to distinguish improper or unhealthy use from use of a medication as prescribed or alcohol in moderation. These include the repeated use of drugs to produce pleasure, alleviate stress, and/or alter or avoid reality. It also includes using prescription drugs in ways other than prescribed or using someone else's prescription. **Addiction** refers to substance use disorders at the severe end of the spectrum and is characterized by a person's inability to control the impulse to use drugs even when there are negative consequences....NIDA uses the term **misuse,** as it is roughly equivalent to the term **abuse**. Substance abuse is a diagnostic term that is increasingly avoided by professionals because it can be shaming, and adds to the stigma that often keeps people from asking for help. Substance misuse suggests use that can cause harm to the user or their friends or family"* (reproducing the quote in italics and for the sake of emphasizing the key terms, we use bold letter replacing the italic lettering used in the NIDA paper) (NIDA, Media Guide July 2018).

14 INTRODUCING MAJOR DRUGS OF ABUSE: HALLUCINOGENS

Hallucinogens is a term used widely for a diverse group of specific natural, known since antiquity, and modern synthetic (man-made) drugs. Specific hallucinogens have been used by some ancient civilizations and cultures as part of religious rituals and ceremonies, as agents for creating mystical experiences and at a minimal level occasionally as remedies for some ailments. They are separated into two categories, namely as classic hallucinogens (such as LSD) and as dissociative drugs (such as PCP which can make users feel out of control or get sensations of being disconnected from their bodies and their environment.).

Stemming from the term 'hallucination', defined by Merriam Webster as *'perception of objects with no reality usually arising from disorder of the nervous system or in response to drugs'*, hallucinogens, when taken, seem to alter the users' awareness of their surroundings as well as their own thoughts and feelings. Classic hallucinogens typically produce visual and auditory hallucinations as users see images, hear sounds and feel sensations which objectively do not exit and may result in an altered sense of time and heightened sensory experiences. The effects of using a hallucinogen start in the span of a little less or a little more than an hour and can last for more than a dozen hours.

Hallucinogens were used in clinical setting during the 20th century. They were simultaneously used and they continue to be used since the last decades of the 20th century and up to today for social, recreational or simply for mood altering purposes. In describing their hallucinogenic experiences users refer to them as *'trips'* and in cases where the effects of using the drug are unpleasant and disturbing users describe them as *'bad trips'*.

The most common classic hallucinogens and dissociative drugs (NIDA April 2019) are:

14.1 CLASSIC HALLUCINOGENS

LSD (D-Lysergic Acid Diethylamide) was initially created in 1938 by Albert Hoffman while he was working in the research laboratories of the Swiss pharmaceutical company Sandoz and in its commonly known form was produced by Hoffman in 1943 when accidentally, aside from the laboratory animals used as experimental subjects, he was the first human who tried it and became aware of its effects on the human brain and nervous system. It is one of the most powerful mind-altering chemicals. It comes as a clear or white odourless material made from lysergic acid, which is found in a fungus that grows on rye and other grains. LSD has many other street names, including acid, blotter acid, dots, and mellow-yellow.

Before we proceed with brief presentations of other *classic hallucinogens* we feel obliged to add a few more words on LSD as it has had a fascinating history from the time it was discovered and used for clinical reasons to the times it was used and continues to be used outside the clinical settings. LSD starting in the 1960's and 1970's continues to be present in global recreational use despite the broadly reported adverse effects on significantly altering and affecting the behaviour of the users endangering their lives and grossly taxing their mental health.

As we have already noted above, LSD was discovered in 1938 by Alfred Hoffman who was seeking the development of a respiratory and circulatory systems stimulant chemical compound. In the process he developed LSD (the expanded name is *Lysergic Acid Diethylamide* which obviously does not correspond to the abbreviated form which originates from the German expansion *Lysergische Säure* D*iethylamide*). After a series of tests were carried through Sandoz decided that the specific substance had no useful results for their pharmacologists and physicians and discontinued further testing.

It was in the middle of the Second World War on April 16, 1943 when Hoffman having resumed his tests with LSD while the compound crystallized into a salt that he suddenly started experiencing very strange feelings forcing him to leave his Lab and return home. Thirteen days later Hoffman produced a dose of LSD and consumed it. The effects, as he described in a 2006 New York Times interview, started less than an hour after consuming his dose and they were: '*dizziness, feeling of anxiety, visual distortions, symptoms of paralysis, desire to laugh*'. The creator of LSD was personally experiencing and living the hallucinogenic and psychedelic effects of his discovery. An extensive story based on Tom Shroder's book titled: 'Acid Test – LSD, Ecstasy and the Power to Heal' appeared on September 9, 2014 in the *Atlantic* with the title '*Apparently Useless: The Accidental Discovery of LSD*' *(Shroder, 2014)*.

Psilocybin (4-phosphoryloxy-N, N-dimethyltryptamine) comes from certain types of mushrooms found in tropical and subtropical regions of South America, Mexico, and the United States. It was originally used by shamans in Mexico and South America and in the mid 1950's the man who discovered and created LSD, Albert Hoffman, isolated it along with the related substance psilocin (also known as psilocyn and psilocine) from Mexican mushrooms. Hoffman determined that psilocybin was the major hallucinogenic component of the mushrooms and psilocin the minor one. Interestingly enough, however, once psilocybin enters the human body it becomes unstable and converts to psilocin which is somewhat more potent than psilocybin. Psilocin is considered to be responsible for the neurological and psychological effects on the users. Some common names used on the Street for psilocybin include little smoke, magic mushrooms, and 'Shrooms'.

Psilocybin and LSD were used in 'mind and conscience expansion experiments' by two Harvard University Psychology Department faculty members Richard Alpert and Timothy Leary who began their experiments in 1960 using volunteer graduate students. Ethical considerations as well as serious criticisms of their methodology intensified a couple of years later ultimately leading to Alpert's immediate dismissal (he was fired in 1963 and Leary was fired shortly after) and they were banned from American Academia. The following paragraph is taken from a Harvard University Department of Psychology page dedicated to Timothy Leary: *'Discredited by their lack of scientific rigor and failure to observe established research guidelines, Timothy Leary and Richard Alpert were both banished from academia, but that was far from the end of their public lives: both men went on to become icons of the psychedelic drug, counterculture, and human potential movement. Leary became famous for the slogan 'Tune in, Turn On, Drop Out'. Alpert, under the name Baba Ram Dass, wrote a popular book called Be Here Now, described as a 'modern spiritual classic'* (Harvard University, Department of Psychology. Timothy Leary

Peyote (mescaline) is a small, spineless cactus (Lophophora williamsii) known for centuries to Mexican and South American natives and used in religious and healing rituals. Mescaline is contained in the cactus' disc shaped buttons located at its top referred to as 'the crown'. Peyote contains the hallucinogenic ingredient mescaline which is extracted from the cactus and can also be produced synthetically. Common names for peyote are buttons, cactus, Mesc and Peyoto.

DMT (N, N-dimethyltryptamine) is a powerful chemical found naturally in some Amazonian plants. Ayahuasca is a tea made from such plants, and when taken in this form it is also known as hoasca, aya, and yagé. Natural DMT comes as a pink, orange or yellow powder. DMT can also be produced as a synthetic drug and usually takes the form of a white crystalline powder that is smoked. DMT is a powerful psychedelic drug used in rituals at various parts of the world. A popular name for synthetic DMT used on the Street by drug pushers is ***Dimitri.*** We call our readers' attention to a special report on DMT published by BBC under the title: *'A DMT trip 'feels like dying' - and scientists now agree'* (Bryant, 14 September 2018).

251-NBOMe is a synthetic hallucinogen with similarities both to LSD and MDMA but is much more potent. Developed for use in brain research, when sold on the street it is sometimes called N Bomb or 251. The summary of a special Report of the World Health Organization on 251-NBOMe published 16-20 June 2014 (page 3) states:

"25I-NBOMe is a substituted phenethylamine and derivative of 2C-I. It is a potent full agonist of the serotonin 5-HT2A receptor in particular and appears to have stimulant and particularly hallucinogenic effects. It has been associated with numerous non-fatal intoxications and some

deaths, with seized material and use reported in many countries. It has been reportedly sold as LSD or as a 'legal' alternative to LSD or "research chemical" usually via Internet websites. The variation in formulations and resultant dosage coupled with its potency results in health risks to the individual. There are no data concerning the abuse or dependence potential of 25INBOMe".

MDMA (Ecstasy or Molly) *3, 4-methylenedioxy-methamphetamine* is a synthetic drug which alters the individual's perception and subjective mood state bearing similar effects on the user of both stimulants and hallucinogens. DMDA is more widely known as *Ecstasy or Molly* and was once associated with night-club entertainment and the so-called 'rave' parties as a psychedelic drug. Ultimately the use of Ecstasy spread outside the night-clubs and is now widely used on a global scale by persons desiring to reach increased levels of energy and pleasure. Etymologically the word 'Ecstasy' derives from the Greek term '*ekstasis - εκστασις* ' meaning '*standing outside oneself*' properly describing the users' subjective experiences of an overwhelming sense of energy and pleasure. When taken orally Ecstasy starts producing the desired psychedelic effects in less than an hour and they last, depending on the individual user's physical and mental conditions, for 3 and up to 6 hours. When the individual users wish to extent the effects of **Ecstasy** they usually take one more pill or tablet before the psychedelic experiences wear-off.

14.2 DISSOCIATIVE DRUGS

PCP (Phencyclidine) was developed in the 1950s as a general anaesthetic for surgery, but it is no longer used for this purpose due to the fact that is has a very long half-time and additionally some serious side effects including hallucinations. PCP can be found in a variety of forms, including tablets or capsules. However, liquid and white crystal powder are the most common forms and since the late 1960's it is used mainly in veterinary practice. PCP is used as an illicit drug and drug pushers and addicts refer to it by various slang names such as Angel Dust, Hog, Love Boat, and Peace Pill (Corssen G, Domino EF 1966).

Ketamine is used as a surgery anaesthetic for humans and animals first introduced into clinical practice in the mid-1960's and considered more useful having less negative side-effects than PCP. Much of the ketamine sold on the streets for illicit use by addicts comes from veterinary offices. It mostly sells as a powder or as pills, but it is also available as an injectable liquid. Ketamine is snorted or sometimes added to drinks as a 'date-rape' drug. Slang names for ketamine include Special K and Cat Valium (Li, L., Vlisides, P.E, 2016).

Dextromethorphan (DXM) is a cough suppressant and mucus-clearing ingredient contained in some over-the-counter cold and cough medicines (syrups, tablets, and gel capsules). It was first produced in the late 1940's by the pharmaceutical company Hoffman-La Roche and granted a patent in 1950. DXM was widely used in the 1960's and 1970's as a 'cheap thrill' drug by addicts who would consume one or two anti-cough bottles (or several pills) in getting 'high'. Robo is a common slang name for DXM used on the street by drug pushers and addicts.

Salvia (Salvia divinorum) is a plant common to southern Mexico and Central and South America belonging to the Lamiaceae mint family used by Mexican shamans in religious and healing rituals. The plant contains opioid-like compounds which produce hallucinations. Salvia is typically ingested by chewing fresh leaves or by drinking their extracted juices as a tea. The dried leaves of salvia can also be smoked or vaporized and inhaled. Popular names for salvia are Diviner's Sage, Maria Pastora, Sally-D, and Magic Mint.

Closing this section we will underline the neurological and chemical differences of effects between the classic hallucinogens and the dissociative hallucinogens. *Classic hallucinogens* affect the human brain by temporarily disrupting communication between brain chemical systems throughout the brain and spinal cord. Some hallucinogens interfere with the action of the brain chemical serotonin, which regulates mood, sensory perception, sleep, hunger, body temperature, sexual behaviour and intestinal muscle control. *Dissociative hallucinogenic* drugs interfere with the action of the brain chemical glutamate, which regulates pain perception, responses to the environment, emotion, learning and memory.

14.3 CANNABIS (MARIJUANA)

An explanatory note is needed here to answer potential questions relating to our presentation of cannabis, a plant that belongs to the Cannabacae family, under the general category of the hallucinogens. There is a plethora of books, scholarly articles, popular Mass Media exposes and editorials classifying cannabis as a 'hallucinogen' due to the fact that the plant, especially the 'cannabis indica' type, among a large number of other cannabinoids contains the hallucinogenic substance known as 'as delta-9-tetrahydrocannabinol' (THC) the main hallucinogenic ingredient which gives the desired 'high' to the users. The other widely known type of the plant the 'cannabis sativa' popularly referred to as 'hemp' has been used through the ages to produce a large variety of products such as ropes, boat sails and textiles.

Cannabis is known on the Street, among drug pushers and users, by a multitude of names among which most predominant seem to be marijuana, hashish, pot, dope, kif, weed, joint, dagga, grass, ganja.

Cannabis has been around for thousands of years, it is assumed to have become known first in India, later on in China and ultimately in Europe. It was introduced to the American continent by Europeans a few centuries ago. It should not be seen and be considered as an exaggeration on our part the suggestion that in simple terms cannabis, especially the *indica* type which contains tetrahydrocannabinol (THC), throughout history on a global scale has been and continues to be one of the most misunderstood widely used and abused substances (Holland, J., MD, 2010; Elliot, S 2011).

Throughout countless centuries and up to our times, Cannabis has had a long history of conflicting attitudes relating to its use and its effects on humans and human behaviour. Eternally there has been and continues to be a part of the public and politicians who condemn it as a drug responsible for the corruption of human beings and especially dangerous for young people leading them to become dependent users. Another part of the public have been and continue to hold a more lenient attitude hailing it as a mild aid in making the user 'feel good', providing the users with the experience of a mild 'high'. Indeed for the so-called 'hippie generation' members marijuana has been seen as a miraculous help in expanding and extending their creativity.

According to the United Nations Office on Drugs and Crime 2019 report cannabis is by far, globally, the most widely cultivated, trafficked and abused illicit drug on every continent and geographic with an estimated 188 million people having used the drug in 2017 (UNODC 2019).

The use of cannabis has seen a 60% rise during the last decade, on a global scale and it is estimated that some 200 million people are regular cannabis users while Europe, according to a report by DW, appears to *be 'home of the highest global concentrations of teenage pot-smokers'*. In the United Kingdom cannabis use is illegal and users face heavy fines and several years of imprisonment, while in the United States and in the European Union cannabis use is in some form legal in some member States and at the same time illegal in others. The treatment of users varies from State to State in the US and from Nation to Nation in the European Union (Roth, DW, 2019).

In the last few years a special interest has focused on the cannabinoids contained in the marijuana plant, but the US Food and Drug Administration (FDA) has not classified it yet as a medical substance. As a rule the FDA requires large scale studies engaging hundreds of thousands of human subjects in order to approve various substances as medicines and up to this point such studies have not been done.

The cannabis plant contains more than a hundred cannabinoids but recently the main interest has been focused on THC (which produces the 'high' to users) and CBD (Cannabidiol) the second in volume cannabinoid found in the plant and their positive medical-therapeutic effects on a variety of health problems. THC appears to decrease nausea, pain, inflammation and muscle control problems. CBD, unlike THC does not produce a 'high' in the user but appears to have analgesic and anti-inflammatory effects, and controls epileptic seizures. The FDA has approved a CBD based medication (brand name *Epidiolex*) for the treatment of two forms of severe childhood epilepsy, namely the Dravet syndrome and the Lennox-Gastaut syndrome (NIDA July 2019).

Peter Grinspoon, MD writing in the Harvard Medical School blog on August 24, 2018 makes an interesting contribution titled *'Cannabidiol (CBD) — what we know and what we don't'* noting that CBD comes mainly from the hemp plant (cannabis sativa not cannabis indica):

"CBD is readily obtainable in most parts of the United States, though its exact legal status is in flux. All 50 states have laws legalizing CBD with varying degrees of restriction, and while the federal government still considers CBD in the same class as marijuana, it doesn't habitually enforce against it" (Grinspoon, updated 2019).

An historic change concerning the prescription of medical cannabis by qualified specialist doctors came into effect on November 1, 2018 in the United Kingdom. For the first time in the UK, expert doctors have been given the option to legally issue prescriptions for cannabis-based medicines when they judge that their patients could benefit from this treatment. Furthermore, the new law do not limit the types of conditions that can be considered for treatment and doctors will no longer need to seek approval from an expert panel in order to enable their patients to access the medicines (Gov.UK 2018).

On a global scale, from North and South America to Europe and Asia many countries have already introduced legislation permitting the medical use of CBD based cannabinoids (including the two co-authors homeland Greece) and the process of legalization is continuing with most resistance encountered in far Eastern countries including China.

In an historic meeting, the World Health Organization (WHO) Expert Committee on Drug Dependence held in Geneva Switzerland 4-7 June 2018 clearly suggested that a review policy on cannabis should be decided in a 'critical review' and relevant medicinal preparations considered to consist of pure CBD should not be scheduled within the International Drug Control Conventions. In its summary the Report states:

"The fortieth ECDD undertook a critical review of cannabidiol (CBD) and pre-reviews of cannabis plant and resin; extracts and tinctures of cannabis; Δ9 -tetrahydrocannabinol (Δ9 -THC); and isomers of THC. The following recommendations were made: Cannabidiol - The Committee recommended that preparations considered to be pure CBD should not be scheduled within the International Drug Control Conventions. Cannabis plant and resin - The Committee concluded that there is sufficient evidence to proceed to a critical review. Extracts and tinctures of cannabis - The Committee concluded that there is sufficient evidence to proceed to a critical review. Δ9 -THC - The Committee concluded that there is sufficient evidence to proceed to a critical review. Tetrahydrocannabinol (Isomers of THC) - the Committee concluded that there is sufficient evidence to proceed to a critical review" (WHO 4-7June 2018).

15 OPIUM: A BRIEF HISTORIC OVERVIEW OF GLOBAL TRADING AND GLOBAL USE

Opium is the Latin rendition of the ancient Greek word 'ὄπιον' originating from and referring to the ancient Greek word 'οπός' meaning 'the juice of a plant'. Opium is extracted in the form of a latex when, after the plant's flower petals have fallen off, incisions are made to the pods which house the seeds of the opium poppy (Papaver somniferum). The latex exuded by the seedpods coagulates as it is exposed to air and turns brownish in colour. The latex can be ground to powder and is usually sold in the form of powder, lump, cake or brick. The opium poppy is a flowering plant of the family of poppies known as Papaveraceae which was and continues to be cultivated since antiquity almost everywhere around the Globe and has been considered both a blessing and a curse for humans and for human societies for several millennia.

There are no physical records relating to the initial extensive use of opium poppy but there appears to be a consensus and it is generally agreed that around 3,400 BC opium was cultivated in lower Mesopotamia (the geographical area between the rivers Tigris and Euphrates corresponding to what is today the Nation of Iraq) by the Sumerian civilization. Sumerian clay tablets describe opium as 'gil' their word for joy and the plant as 'Hul Gil' (meaning 'joy plant') indicating that Sumerians had recognized its 'euphoric' properties as a drug. However, it is not clear if there was a widespread use. It is assumed that opium and its use was passed on from the Sumerians to the Assyrians, then on to Babylonians and ultimately to the Egyptians.

The Egyptians, by 1,500 BC appear to have cultivated the opium poppy in vast quantities especially in the city of 'Thebes' located in Upper Egypt and extracted from it an alkaloid to which they gave the name 'Thebaine' originating from the city's Greek name 'Thebes' (' Θῆβαι' in Greek). *Thebaine* which produces stimulatory effects, is chemically similar to two other opium alkaloids, namely *morphine* and *codeine* which have more potent depressant effects on the human nervous system. Opium usage dressed in a cloud of mystical qualities was encountered in ancient Greece and Rome and with the expansion of the Roman Empire was ultimately passed on to the rest of the European continent.

For many centuries AD opium was widely used by medical men and pharmacists as a potent analgesic administered to minimize the pain suffered by ordinary men, women and children and also to ease the excruciating pain experienced by wounded soldiers. It is widely accepted that Arab traders between the 8th and 10th centuries AD introduced opium to China where it was extensively used taken either orally or through smoking. Originally, the Portuguese were the prime suppliers of opium to China through the port of Canton but ultimately the trade of opium to China came under the control of the British while an estimated 10% of all trade was done by Americans. An interesting analysis of the trade of opium to the Chinese is available in a two part series at Radio Station WBUR titled *'How Profits from Opium Shaped 19th Century Boston'* (Bebinger July 31, August 1, 2017*)*.

During the second half of the 18th century the Beijing Central Government alarmed by the huge numbers of the Chinese population becoming addicted to opium use introduced a number of restrictions. Despite the imposed restrictions the British owned *East India Company* (EIC) continued to ship to their warehouses located in the area of the port city of Canton vast amounts of opium. Shortly before the end of the 18th century, the sale of opium was declared illegal. During the early 19th century The East India Company kept shipping vast amounts of opium to its warehouses in the Canton area from where smugglers were selling opium farther in mainland China providing impressive gains for the EIC. The East India Company monopoly in the Chinese opium market had ceased during the 1830's but it continued to send opium to Canton as did several other companies from various other Nations. In this respect while the majority of opium quantities brought to Canton and sold in China were still controlled by British interests, very large quantities of opium were sold to the Chinese by American companies who would buy opium from an impressive number of producers located in Turkey and then ship it to China.

In the late 1830's, the Qing Dynasty realizing that the opium brought to Canton and then sold farther inland by smugglers had deleterious effects on the health of the Chinese people who were becoming addicted in large numbers and catastrophic effects on the economy, decided to ban the import of opium. Two so-called 'opium wars' ensued. The first between the Chinese and British (1839-1842) and the second between the Chinese and British-French Allied Forces (1856-1858).

In 1839 the Qing Dynasty ordered a local official to blockade the British opium carrying ships in the Canton Harbour until they agreed to hand over their cargo. The British took this action as an insult to the Crown and dispatched a fleet under the command of Admiral Charles Elliott 'to teach the Chinese a proper lesson'. In the war that followed lasting from 1839 to 1842 British technological superiority smashed the Chinese defences and ended with the signing of the Nanjing Treaty of 1842 which resulted in handing over Hong Kong Island to the British and allowed continuation of the trade and the access of Missionaries to inland Chinese territories.

In 1856, following the eruption of a Chinese civil war, Yeh Ming-ch'en, a man who loathed the foreigner's exploitation of the free trade zone of Canton and was determined to stamp out the opium trade and the corruption of the Chinese people was appointed Imperial Commissioner of the Canton Province. One of his first acts was to seize the British ship *Arrow* and imprison its crew. The British Governor of Hong Kong called in the British Fleet which bombarded Chinese fortifications and later on some Chinese controlled parts of the city but he did not have the necessary military means to seize Canton. In December of 1856 as a series of riots erupted, European commercial properties were destroyed by fire and a French missionary was brutally killed. With the support of the French forces Britain obliged the Chinese in June 1858 into signing the *Treaty of Tientsin*, also known as the *Treaty of Tianjin* ratified by the Chinese Emperor in 1860. The Treaty effectively legalized opium trade, opened up more access cities and ports to foreigners and foreign trade, permitted massive Christian missionary activities and created the Beijing Legation Quarter which was the area where various foreign legations (lower in rank than Embassies) were established in the span of almost a century from1861 to 1959.

Closing the above brief references to the two China-Britain and China-Britain/France Opium Wars we call your attention to a straightforward and critical editorial by Karl E. Meyer published on June 28, 1997 in the New York Times on the occasion of the historic return of Hong Kong to China (Meyer, June 28, 1997).

If you as our readers and we as the authors of this book were living in Beijing in the year 1861, we would have witnessed various foreign legations settling in the Chinese capital city. If during that same year we would have decided to leave behind the Chinese coastal line and by crossing the Pacific Ocean on a steamship we would reach California about 5 to 6 weeks later we would witness the onset of the bloody American Civil War (1861-1865). During that time period we would also become witnesses to the rampant administration and use of opium and opioids for easing the pains of the countless wounded soldiers of both the Union and the Confederate Armies. The widespread practice of administering opium and opioids created the first opioid crisis in the USA. The second USA opioid crisis is unfolding as you are reading our book.

The widespread dispersion of opium pills and morphine injections to wounded soldiers of the American Civil War is discussed by Erick Trickey in his article published January 4, 2018 in the Smithsonian titled: *'Inside the Story of America's 19th-Century Opiate Addiction'*. The author notes that millions of opium pills and millions of opium powders and tinctures were administered to members of the Union Army creating countless numbers of soldiers returning home as addicts to opium and opioids. The author notes that the use of opium in the United States is almost as old as the Nation itself emerging as a widespread practice during the American Revolution period when both Continental and British armies administered opium to wounded and to sick soldiers (Trickey, January 4, 2018).

Closing we will note that a variety of 'street' names are used by addicts and dealers for *opium* including Ah-Pen-Yen, Auntie, Aunt Emma, Big O, Black, Black Pill, Black Russian (opium mixed with hashish), Chandoo, China, Chinese Molasses, Chinese Tobacco, Chocolate, Cruz, Dopium, Dover's Powder, Dream Gum, Dream Stick, Dreams, Easing Powder, Fi-Do-Nie, Gee, God's Medicine, Goma, Gondola, Goric, Great Tobacco, Gum, Guma, Hocus, Hops, Incense, Joy Plant, Midnight Oil, Mira, Ope, Opio, Pen Yan, Pin Gon, Pin Yen, Pox, Skee, Toxy, Toys, When-Shee and Zero.

15.1 OPIATES

We chose *Opiates* as our label for this section and not the modern label *Opioids* simply out of respect for observing the historically significant labelling classification process. The modern label Opioids includes all O*piates* (natural products emanating from Opium or semi-synthetic products with opium origin) as well as all other addictive synthetic drugs such as Oxycodone, Hydrocodone, Fentanyl and Methadone. We are fully aware of the reality that nowadays as the classification O*piates* seems to be fading away O*pioids* is becoming increasingly dominant as it describes all drugs, natural and synthetic, which relate to and act on opioid receptors in humans.

Early in the 17th century a tincture of opium (an extract of 10% opium powder dissolved in ethanol, i.e. ethyl-alcohol or distilled spirits such as whiskey), named **'*laudanum*'** and containing most of the opium alkaloids, including morphine and codeine, was introduced into medical practice by the English physician Thomas Sydenham as a pain relieving medication and cough suppressant (Encyclopaedia Britannica, Thomas Sydenham).

A forceful account vividly describing the pleasures and pains of using an opiate came as a personal, autobiographical confession of dependence on 'laudanum' and appeared in September and October 1821 anonymously in the London Magazine. The next year, 1822 it was published as a book bearing the title *'Confessions of a British Opium Eater and Other Essays'* authored by Thomas De Quincy. Among literary historians it is widely held that this book, the first of its kind as an autobiographical account on drug dependence, secured almost instant recognition for De Quincy and has ever since been acclaimed as a precursor to newer similar novels and treatises.

Viewing matters in an historical perspective, it should be noted that the Swiss physician and alchemist (who was born as Philippus Aureolus Theophrastus Bombastus von Hohenheim but assumed the name *Paracelsus* by which he is known ever since*)* had created in the 16th century a pain killing medication composed of a variety of substances but also containing opium to which he gave the name *laudanum* (Ball, 2006).

With the onset of the 18ᵗʰ century Jacob Le Mort, a professor of chemistry at Leiden University in the Netherlands created a *'camphorated tincture of opium'* having antitussive as well as analgesic capabilities and aimed it as a special remedy for asthma. He gave to his creation the name *'paregoric'* using the ancient Greek word for 'soothing' or 'consoling' pain (in ancient Greek 'παρηγορικός' and in modern Greek 'παρηγορητικός'). Paregoric ever since its creation has been used in treating a variety of conditions and also as an antidiarrheal medication.

Paregoric is a 'tincture of opium' but it should not be confused with the other 'tincture of opium' *laudanum* which contains almost twenty five times more morphine than does paregoric.

At the start of the 19ᵗʰ century, between 1803 -1805, a German pharmacist and pioneer in alkaloid chemistry research named Friedrich Wilhelm Adam Sertürner, living and practicing in the city of Paderborn, isolated from opium an alkaloid in crystalline form as a crystal structure. He gave to the alcaloid the name *'morphium'* from Morpheus (etymologically Μορφέας) the ancient Greek God of sleep. He did so as he discovered that this new substance eased pain and induced painless sleep when administered to stray dogs and ultimately to humans in controlled dosages. Sertürner's opiate, the crystalline alkaloid *'morphium'*, ultimately came to be known globally as *'morphine'*.

Morphine was produced and marketed commercially in 1827 by Merck Pharmaceutical Laboratories located in Darmstadt, Germany. It was medically administered to patients in the form of liquid solutions or pills. Following the invention of the *hypodermic syringe* (the word derives etymologically from the ancient Greek word σύριγξ, the contemporary Greek σύριγγα meaning a tube) *morphine* begun to be administered to patients hypodermically. Indeed in the last two centuries it has been and continues to be used on a global scale as an almost *'magical cure'*. Morphine eases not only the excruciating pains suffered by soldiers wounded in various Battlefields, but also of all other persons suffering from pain relating to a variety of causes and ailments including in the course of the last few decades cancer patients (Courtwright, 2001).

Delving into the history of syringes it emerges that an Irish physician named Francis Rynd invented the hollow needle and used it to make the first recorded subcutaneous injections in 1844. Shortly thereafter in 1853 Charles Pravaz and Alexander Wood developed a medical hypodermic syringe with a needle fine enough to pierce the skin. In the second half of the 20ᵗʰ century and up to now a prevalent form of inexpensive, single use, hypodermic syringes is the plastic one. These types of 'cheap' plastic syringes are widely used by drug addicts not for a single shot but among their group members thus spreading among them a variety of diseases such as HIV and Hepatitis C. In 1974 the African American inventor Phil Brooks received a US patent for his 'Disposable Syringe' (Omnisurge, May 5, 2015).

Some 'street' names used by addicts and dealers for *morphine* are: Dreamer, First Line, God's Drug, Joy Juice, Miss Emma, Monkey, Mister Blue, Morpho, Unkie, and White Stuf.

Codeine also called 'methyl morphine' was discovered in 1832 by the French pharmacist and chemist Pierre-Jean Robiquet as an alkaloid that can be extracted directly from opium. Later on and currently it is produced from morphine. After its discovery it was originally used as a mild analgesic pain reliever and cough suppressant. It continues to be used in many cough syrups.

Academics and craftsmen know that discoveries of new artefacts, new processes and new products emerge as the creative, inspirational addition to or improvement of already existing ones which have been produced earlier by scientists and other craftsmen. In this realm, and as we come to close this section on opiates (opioids), we will make a brief, virtual stop at St. Mary's Hospital Medical School in London in the year 1874 and introduce you to the work of Charles Romley Alder Wright, a Lecturer in Chemistry and Physics and founder of the Royal Institute of Chemistry of Great Britain.

Searching for non-addictive alternatives to widely used *morphine* Wright experimented in combining *morphine* with a variety of acids and in 1874 he produced a more potent, acetylated form of morphine referred to as '*diacetylmorphine* or *morphine diacetate*'. Twenty three years later, the German chemist Felix Hoffman, working at Bayer's pharmaceutical laboratory under the auspices of Professor Heinrich Dresser, created the *acetylsalicylic acid*, namely the drug known as 'aspirin'. Subsequently Dresser instructed Hoffman to acetylate morphine with the objective of producing a new form of codeine. In the process Hoffman came to re-invent Wright's creation of *diacetylmorphine* which administered to patients on equal dosages was much more potent than morphine. Legally, though, the new product due to Wright's work was not patentable by Bayer (Science History Institute, Felix Hoffmann).

In the excitement of the discovery of a new drug for treating cough and controlling pain, obviously more potent and hence more effective than morphine, Friedrich Bayer & Co. the German Pharmaceutical Company, gave to the new product the brand name **Heroin** and started selling it in 1898. It should be noted here that as persons who were administered the new drug responded that beyond its anti-cough and pain-killing properties it gave them a sense of euphoria and elation. The name *Heroin* was borrowed from the German word *Heroisch* which in English means *Heroic* and etymologically originates from the Greek word Hero ('ήρωας' denoting a person who has done something great and admirable, or in other words a brave man).

There are several 'street' names for *Heroin* in the addicts' world created by dealers in their attempts to escape Police detection of their 'merchandise'. In English speaking countries some such 'street names' are H, Big H, Brown Sugar, Brown, Beast, Hell Dust, Horse, Junk (hence the addict's nick-name 'junkie') Nose Drops, Smack, Thunder, Dope, Skag, Snow, Horse, China white, Hero.

During the first years of marketing *Heroin* as a new drug, Bayer claimed that it had discovered not only a better and, when administered in equal doses, a much more potent drug than the classic morphine, but indeed a revolutionary drug which when properly administered by physicians could liberate humans from their 'addiction bondage' to *morphine*. As it later turned out *Heroin* was destined to become humanity's menace and its official production from Bayer ceased around 1913 when the new drug's more serious addictive characteristics were discovered.

Subsequently the numbers of heroin addicts begun to swell globally to unprecedented numbers and many Nations started introducing legislation forbidding its sale. However, due to colossal demand from addicts, when legal production ceased, its illegal production was taken over by what was called '*The French Connection*'. The process of smuggling heroin from France to New York was described in Robin Moore's 1969 non-fiction book titled 'The French Connection'. The script of the same title 1971 movie was based on Moore's book and during the 44th Academy Awards won 4 Oscars including the Oscar for best movie while protagonist Gene Hackman won the Oscar for best actor. The route followed by criminal gangs involved smuggling raw heroin from Turkey to Marseille, France and after refinement shipping it off to the USA. This operation was smashed in the 1970's but by that time similar operations adjacent to the Southern borders of the United States had already sprang up in Mexico (Robin Moore, 1969; Wikipedia, The French Connection-film).

Methadone is a synthetic opioid which was discovered in Germany in the late 1930's shortly before WWII and credited to two German scientists Max Bockmühl and Gustav Ehrhart who at that time were working for the German pharmaceutical company Hoechst, AG. The new synthetic opioid was to be used as an analgesic by German troops during the War. In 1941 the two researchers, as has been verified by relevant documents, applied for a patent for their substance called '*Hoechst 10820*'. It should be noted here that a predecessor to *Methadone* given the name of **Pethidine** was created at Hoechst Laboratories in 1938-1939 and considered less addictive than *Morphine* as a pain-killer but it had a much shorter drastic effect and a shorter duration. After the end of WWII in 1947 the rights to production and sale of *Methadone* were taken over by the American drug manufacturing company Elli Lilly & Co. and *Methadone* started to be marketed in the United States under the new name of *Dolophine* (Payne, J.T. 1991).

A myth was circulating in the 1960's and 1970's among addicts in the USA associated with Methadone's marketing brand-name *Dolophine* implying that the drug was named after Adolph Hitler (*Adolophine*). The more plausible reality is that the name is a synthesis of the Latin word *'dolor'* (in French doleur) meaning *pain* and Latin word for *end* 'finis' (in French fin).

The use of *methadone* as a substitute for heroin leading ultimately to the end of dependence and addiction to *heroin* when properly administered in methadone programs, is credited to the pioneering work of Drs Vincent Dole, the late Marie Nyswander and Mary Jeanne Kreek which commenced in 1964. *Methadone* as a substitute drug for heroin was experimentally applied from 1958 to 1962 at the USPHS hospital in Lexington, at the Bellevue Medical Center in New York City, and at a limited number of other sites for 'detoxification' treatment of *heroin* addiction (Dole, VP, Nyswander, ME, and Kreek, MJ. 1966).

Buprenorphine is a synthetic opioid medication that acts as a partial agonist at opioid receptors. The drug does not produce the euphoria and sedation caused by the use of heroin or other opioids but it is effective in reducing or even eliminating withdrawal symptoms associated with opioid dependence. A significant pharmacological characteristic of Buprenorphine is that it has a minimal potential for overdose.

Buprenorphine is available to be taken sublingually in pure form or as *Suboxone* a specially prescribed formulation which combines *Buprenorphine* with *Naloxone*, an antagonist (or blocker) of opioid receptors. As the relevant National Institute on Drug Abuse (NIDA) on-line report indicates, *Naloxone* has no effect when *Suboxone* is taken as prescribed, but if an addicted individual attempts to inject *Suboxone*, the *Naloxone* will produce severe withdrawal symptoms. Thus, this formulation lessens the likelihood that the drug will be abused or diverted to others.

The drug is also available as in an implant and in liquid form for injection. The U.S. Food and Drug Administration (FDA) approved a 6-month subdermal buprenorphine implant in May 2016 and, as reported in a special press release of the US Food and Drug Administration (FDA) as a once-monthly injection in November 2017 (FDA November 30, 2017).

16 COCAINE

Cocaine is an alkaloid, the best known one of the many alkaloids contained in the coca plant which grows native in South America. The coca plant (*Erythroxylum coca* belongs to the family of *Erythroxylaceae*) and contains *cocaine*. The coca plant was known to the Inca civilization which had occupied for several centuries the geographic areas of the Andes including the geopolitical areas known today as the Nations of Peru and Colombia. Residents of the Andes used coca as far back as 1,000 years BC both for ritualistic as well as medicinal purposes. It has been surmised that chewing coca leaves and ingesting *cocaine* helped the users to deal effectively with a number of specific problems ranging from dealing with the thin oxygen supply in the atmosphere of the Andean region's high elevation, to restoring gastrointestinal balance and lessening the sense of hunger. Needless to say surely there were those users who simply sought the euphoria and elation produced by cocaine (Biondich, A.S., and Joslin, J.D., 2016).

After 1532 when the Spaniards invaded and subdued the Incas, the conquerors attempted to control and eradicate the use of coca by the indigenous population, but as their efforts proved unsuccessful in curtailing patterns of behaviour established for many centuries they decided instead to exploit the cultivation of coca plants. Indeed, they engaged in the custom of providing agricultural workers with a ration of coca leaves in addition to their wages. Ultimately, coca use became even more widespread among the people of the former Incan empire and continues to be currently part of the life and behaviour patterns of Andean workers (Stolberg, V, B. 2011).

The Spanish conquistadores (or conquistadors) slowly introduced the coca plants to Europe over the course of the ensuing couple of centuries. Europeans learned to chew the coca leaves up to the late 19th century while seeking to achieve the sense of euphoria they brought to the users.

In 1853, Heinrich Wackenroder, a German pharmaceutical chemist was the first to produce a crude extract of the active ingredient of coca leaves. Two years later another pharmacist, Friedrich Gaedecke, evaporated an aqueous extract of the leaves and then dried the residue to obtain white crystals, albeit contaminated by an oily residue. He christened them *erythroxyline*, after their botanical source, the shrub E*rythroxyla* coca. In 1860 Albert Niemann reported the first quantitative investigation of the extract, which he called *Cocaine* and was initially used in medical practice in the early 1880's. *Cocaine* was considered by some to be an antidote to morphine dependency and addiction. At the same time cocaine was made available to the public as an elixir creating euphoria and providing the users with increased energy, invigoration and improved and accelerated brain activity (Dronsfield, A. and Ellis, P. 2007).

Cocaine is used in select surgical operations as a local anaesthetic but its use for recreational purposes is illegal. Some of you are probably already familiar with the fact that in Street use the drug cocaine looks like a fine, white crystal powder. Street dealers, in order to increase their profits, often mix it with other substances including other drugs such as amphetamine and synthetic opioids, including fentanyl. Adding synthetic opioids to cocaine renders the mixture especially risky and it is believed that increasing overdose deaths from cocaine use have to do with such tampered cocaine. Cocaine as a powder is smoked, used nasally (snorting), rubbed onto the gums and for more immediate results a liquid solution is injected into the blood stream. Injecting or smoking cocaine produces a quicker and stronger but shorter-lasting 'high' than snorting. Indeed, while the 'high' experienced from snorting cocaine may last 15 to 30 minutes, the high from smoking may last 5 to 10 minutes. Depending on the method of using cocaine some long term effects are: for snorting: loss of smell, nosebleeds, frequent runny nose, and problems with swallowing; for smoking: cough, asthma, respiratory distress, and higher risk of infections like pneumonia; when consuming by mouth: severe bowel decay from reduced blood flow. The use of injection carries problems related to HIV and Hepatitis C if the syringe is not used only by the person injecting his shot. Even in cases of one-use syringes the users risk skin or soft tissue infections, as well as scarring or collapsed veins (NIDA, drug facts, cocaine 2018).

In the Inca civilization coca was reserved for royalty and to a similar fashion since the 19th century European members of the artistic, intellectual, financial, political and even religious 'elites' showed a strong 'appetite' for consuming cocaine contained in the coca plant leaves. Cocaine like heroin and to a lesser degree nicotine affects the brain's 'reward systems' bringing forth elation, self-confidence, extended endurance at work and sexual prowess.

In 1863 an Italian chemist named Angelo Mariani brought to the market a new type of wine called 'Vin Mariani' which had been treated with coca leaves and which brought to its inventor huge financial gains. In a lengthy article in the Independent Paul Vallely wrote: 'Pope Leo XIII conferred on it the gold medal. Writers like Henrik Ibsen, Emile Zola, Jules Verne, Alexander Dumas, and Sir Arthur Conan Doyle were all mad for it. Robert Lewis Stephenson wrote the Strange Case of Dr Jekyll and Mr Hyde during a six day cocaine binge. Royalty were enthusiasts. Queen Victoria, King George of Greece, King Alphonse XIII of Spain, the Shah of Persia and US Presidents William McKinley and Ulysses S. Grant all knocked it back.' In the same lengthy article a reference is made to Sigmund Freud's paper on cocaine "Ueber Coca" written in German where the father of psychoanalysis has commented that cocaine brings 'exhilaration and lasting euphoria, which in no way differs from the normal euphoria of the healthy person...' (Vallely, 2006).

Sigmund Freud's involvement with cocaine deserves a brief treatment at this point. It appears that Freud became aware of cocaine's effects as a 'miracle' drug in curing a variety of ailments and helping free persons addicted to morphine, which had previously been marketed as a 'miracle' pain controlling drug. Writing in the Pharmaceutical Journal (of the Royal Pharmaceutical Society) in December 2000 under the title 'Freud, Sherlock Holmes and Coca Cola: the cocaine connection' Ray Sturgess notes that in 1863, while in his late 20's, Freud became interested in cocaine as he was struggling to make a living and repay his debts. Dr Ernst Von Fleischl-Marxow, who had lend money to Freud was struggling with his morphine addiction acquired after an amputation of his thumb. Unable to pay back his friend Freud saw in cocaine a chance of achieving two goals, namely curing his friend and financial benefactor from his morphine addiction, and proving the usefulness of the 'miracle' drug cocaine. Freud tried the drug on himself, then tried it on his friend who ultimately died never cured from his morphine addiction and Freud found himself bound to the continuous use of cocaine (Sturgess, R, 2000).

Howard Markel in his book titled 'An Anatomy of Addiction: Sigmund Freud, William Halsted, and the Miracle Drug Cocaine' presents a different understanding of the involvement of the father of psychoanalysis Sigmund Freud with cocaine and, essentially, makes the thesis that his experiences with the drug alter his career path as a neurologist shifting his interests from studying the human brain to studying and analysing the human psyche. The description of Markel's book states: 'it tells the tragic and heroic story of each man, accidentally struck down in his prime by an insidious malady: tragic because of the time, relationships, and health cocaine forced each to squander; heroic in the intense battle each man waged to overcome his affliction as he conquered his own world with his visionary healing gifts. Here is the full story, long overlooked, told in its rich historical context' (Markel, P. 2011).

While Cocaine comes in powder form and is usually snorted, **Crack cocaine** comes in the form of solid blocks of crystal appearing in a variety of colors. The crystals are heated and then smoked (the name derives from the cracking sound the crystals make while heated). Crack cocaine is much more potent than Cocaine, and as it is smoked and not snorted has a much more immediate but less lasting effect than Cocaine. Contrary to Cocaine which has a high price (hence its characterization as the 'rich peoples' drug') it is sold at a much lower price which makes it more readily available to teenagers. The reality is that Crack Cocaine has a much more potent addictive effect and so the low price appeal is wiped off once the addicted persons need more daily dosages, thus increasing the amount of money needed in order to satisfy their habit.

16.1 STIMULANTS (AMPHETAMINE AND METHAMPHETAMINE)

Amphetamine and Methamphetamine (known by street names as speed, ice, upper, crystal, chalk, crank, crypto, fire, meth, etc.) is a synthetic stimulant drug which was invented over a century ago and initially used for a variety of medical reasons and also by persons seeking the sense of euphoria, increased levels of alertness and energy. Eventually the free purchase of the drug was legally stopped. Currently it is specifically medically used to treat the condition in children known as *'Attention-deficit hyperactivity disorder'* (ADHD). Amphetamine and methamphetamine not prescribed by a medical doctor but acquired in the drug market by pushers to be used for recreational purposes comes as pills, capsules, powder, crystal and liquid.

Amphetamine's effects in energizing the body and providing improved mental awareness levels has led to the drug's recreational use as a night-club drug especially during the end of the 20th century and up to our times. The use of amphetamine and especially the more potent form of methamphetamine has not been grossly curtailed despite warnings for its potential harmful effects as its euphoric and energizing potential exceeds in intensity and duration the effects experienced by the use of Cocaine and may lead to addictive dependence.

The use of **methamphetamine** and **Ecstasy** has been and continues to be prevalent in East and South-East Asia and appears to be growing in parts of North America and Europe. As the 2015 Report of the United Nations Office on Drugs and Crime (UNODC) points out methamphetamine dominates the global growing and diversifying illicit market for synthetic drugs (UNODC Report 2015).

17 LEGAL AND ILLEGAL USE OF PRESCRIPTION ANTI-ANXIETY DRUGS

As countless millions of people primarily in western types of industrially developed societies as well as in economically less developed countries across the Globe suffer from anxiety a series of specialized medically prescribed 'anti-anxiety' drugs have been developed and are routinely dispensed daily by qualified physicians.

The most commonly prescribed anxiety reducing drugs are the so-called **Benzodiazepines** (also known in the Street as 'benzos') which have greatly replaced barbiturates and are globally known by their brand-marketing names as *Xanax* (alprazolam), *Librium* (chlordiazepoxide) and *Valium* (diazepam). The reality as exposed in Mass Media news stories and editorials is that these drugs are addictive if used over long period of time (extending beyond the usual medical personnel suggestion of up to 4 months).

Ordinary anxiety suffering individuals have become addicted to these drugs while 'addicts', i.e. individuals suffering from substance abuse disorder, prefer to use them instead of alcohol when they cannot have access to opiates or other illicit substances they are dependent on. Benzodiazepines are marketed and dispersed for oral use as tablets and capsules, as well as in the form of sublingual pills or as fluids hypodermically injected.

18 TREATMENT MODALITIES OF INDIVIDUALS WITH SUBSTANCE USE DISORDER (SUD)

Assuming, and hoping you as readers of our book will not object if we assume the proverbial poetic license or freedom in making an analogy, we will state that as each one of us as an individual human being growing up carves his or her own personality and chooses his or her path in society, each individual with substance use disorder carves with his or her experiences the path leading to addiction to some substance.

Surely each drug dependent person deciding to seek help from a private or public drug addiction specialist, physician or therapist, or visiting an outpatient or residential treatment program merits and surely will be provided with a careful review and assessment of his or her problem. Nowadays, in general terms, all SUD persons seeking help and treatment will be faced with the ultimately personal choice of an existing broad spectrum of therapeutic approaches.

As we did in part one and part two of our book in our presentation of the therapeutic approaches available to individuals with alcohol use disorder (AUD) and the behavioural addiction of '*disordered gambling*', we will present below the treatment modalities for persons with substance use disorder (SUD). There is a broad spectrum of drug addiction therapeutic modalities which adhere to a 3-stage progression starting with detoxification, progression to achieving full abstinence and ending with re-entry of an ex-addict into his or her community.

Individuals with SUD, depending on a number of their socio-psychological and financial characteristics can enter a person-to-person relationship with a physician or drug therapist or enrol in a small group program combining counselling and, depending on their needs, use of relevant medication (if needed) while passing through the detoxification process.

Individuals can opt to enter an outpatient day program or a residential live-in program. They can join some type of modality based on the philosophy of 'mutual support' groups using the '12 Step' and the '12 Traditions' approach or the administration of treatment drugs such as Methadone, Buprenorphine (which are erroneously considered as 'substitutes' and not treatment drugs) and Naltrexone. Some short term types of out-patient treatment may require for their successful completion commitment lasting up to 6 months, and finally, they can choose to be admitted to a 'therapeutic community' modality which now lasts from 6-12 months while earlier it lasted up to 24 months (NIDA January 2018).

18.1 NARCOTICS ANONYMOUS (NA) – A 'MUTUAL SUPPORT' FELLOWSHIP MODALITY

Narcotics Anonymous (NA) was formally established in July, 1953 in Van Nuys, Sun Valley, California by 'Jimmy K.' and a group of several individuals who participated in Alcoholics Anonymous meetings. Van Nuys remains the home base of Narcotics Anonymous since 1953. 'Jimmy K.' was a pseudonym used in accordance with AA rules protecting the anonymity of participants. 'Jimmy K.' (1911-1985) was born as James Patrick Kinnon in Scotland before his family moved to the USA and is considered the principal founder of NA. 'Jimmy K.' had started attending AA meeting in 1950 and was doing well until in 1953 he saw, as did some other AA participants, the need to go beyond the battle for recovery and abstinence from alcohol and create the proper program for dealing with dependency on other addictive substances. He never claimed to be the founder of the NA but there appears to be ample evidence pointing to his founding role in giving birth to the Narcotics Anonymous '12 Step' program. 'Jimmy K.' and the small group of fellow Alcoholics Anonymous participants, reportedly 4 men and two women, started holding their meetings as Narcotics Anonymous and manage to secure the AA's permission to adapt and use the '12 Steps' program and the '12 Traditions' created by AA. 'Jimmy K.' succeeded in changing Step 1 of the original AA text to read from *'admitting to be powerless over alcohol'* to the NA appropriate *'admitting to be helpless over addiction'*.

From its humble beginnings in early 1950's Narcotics Anonymous has grown to be present globally today in 144 countries where some 70,000 meetings are regularly held. Narcotics Anonymous books and pamphlets are currently available in 55 languages while translations are in progress in 16 additional languages. Since NA as does AA operates as a voluntary fellowship and carefully protects participants' anonymity, statistical information on actual membership is hard to come by. However, as was announced in the 2015 annual NA world meeting in Rio de Janeiro, Brazil, in a survey in which nearly 23,000 participants responded it was noted that in terms of gender current worldwide membership consists of 59% males and 41% females. In terms of Age 1% are 20 years old and under, 11% are 21–30 years old, 21% are 31–40 years old, 24% are 41–50 years old, 29% are 51-60 years old, and 14% are over 60 years old. In terms of Ethnicity, 74% of the fellowship are Caucasian, 11% African-American, 6% Hispanic, and 9% other (NA 2006-2018).

We recommend to readers of our book wishing to have more detailed information on the NA's history to consult the 6th edition of the 'Narcotics Anonymous' book published in 2008 by the Narcotics Anonymous World Service Office headquartered in Van Nuys, California. The book contains a lot of information on the fellowship's birth and development since the 1950's. 'Jimmy K.' was instrumental in gathering information and personal experience accounts from numerous participants in the fellowship in the creation in early 1960's of NA's *'Little White Book'* also referred to as *'The White Book'* which was, and continues to be used in each and every meeting of NA across the Globe (Narcotics Anonymous 2008).

18.2 THE THERAPEUTIC USE OF DRUGS: METHADONE, BUPRENORPHINE AND NALTREXONE

We have presented Methadone earlier in this part of our book and it should suffice here to emphasize that as an opioid agonist it prevents withdrawal symptoms, reduces craving in opioid-addicted individuals and it is successful in blocking the effects of illicit opioids. Methadone is taken orally and has already had a long history of use in treatment of opioid dependence in adults. The use of Methadone is greatly enhancing its positive effects when combined with some psychotherapeutic support provided individually or in group settings either in the form of counselling or as behavioural therapy such as Cognitive Behavioral Therapy (BCT).

We have also presented Buprenorphine earlier in this part of our book and we should emphasize here that Buprenorphine treatment for detoxification and/or maintenance can be provided in office-based settings by qualified physicians who have received a waiver from the Drug Enforcement Administration (DEA), allowing them to prescribe and administer it. The availability of office-based treatment for opioid addiction is a cost-effective approach that increases the reach of treatment and the options available to patients.

Before we bring forth in our current discussion the use of Naltrexone we feel obliged to bring to our readers' attention an emphatic statement made on a relevant on-line NIDA report:

*"**Treatment, not Substitution**: Because methadone and buprenorphine are themselves opioids, some people view these treatments for opioid dependence as just substitutions of one addictive drug for another. But taking these medications as prescribed allows patients to hold jobs, avoid street crime and violence, and reduce their exposure to HIV by stopping or decreasing injection drug use and drug-related high-risk sexual behavior. Patients stabilized on these medications can also engage more readily in counselling and other behavioral interventions essential to recovery"* (NIDA January 2018).

Naltrexone is a synthetic opioid antagonist we mentioned earlier in the first part of our book while discussing anti-alcohol drugs. This drug blocks opioids from binding to their receptors and thereby prevents their euphoric and other effects. It has been used for many years to reverse opioid overdose and is also approved for treating opioid addiction. The theory behind this treatment is that the repeated absence of the desired effects and the perceived futility of abusing opioids will gradually diminish craving and addiction. Naltrexone itself has no subjective effects following detoxification (that is, a person does not perceive any particular drug effect), it has no potential for abuse, and it is not addictive.

Naltrexone as a treatment for opioid addiction is usually prescribed in outpatient medical settings, although the treatment should begin after medical detoxification in a residential setting in order to prevent withdrawal symptoms. The drug must be taken orally, either daily or three times a week, but noncompliance with treatment is a commonly reported problem. The consensus among experienced clinicians is that Naltrexone is best suited for highly motivated, recently detoxified patients who desire total abstinence because of their personal conditions such as individuals who are employed professionals or recent parolees. Recently, a long-acting injectable version of naltrexone, called Vivitrol, was approved to treat opioid addiction. Because it only needs to be delivered once a month, it facilitates compliance and offers an alternative for those who do not wish to be placed on agonist/partial agonist medications.

18.3 THE THERAPEUTIC COMMUNITY (TC) MODALITY: 'SYNANON' AND 'CONCEPT' TYPE TC'S

Before we make a brief presentation of the *Therapeutic Community* (TC) as a residential, strictly structured, mutual help and support modality for the treatment of drug addicts we will make a brief reference to 'Synanon'. We do so because 'Synanon' is considered by some as the primeval form of a therapeutic community offering treatment to substance dependent persons (originally combining alcoholics and drug addicts) and finally focusing only on drug addicts.

There is no consensus concerning the origin and meaning of the term Synanon but is a fact that the 'Synanon Foundation' was incorporated by its founder Charles "Chuck" Dederich in 1958 in the city of Santa Monica, California aiming to be a two year 'mutual support' residential fellowship for the treatment of drug addicts. Dederich an ex-alcoholic member of the AA fellowship, resisted the AA's exclusion of drug addicts from the '12-Step' fellowship program.

As Richard Ofshe noted in his 1980 article in 'Sociological Analysis' titled 'The Social Development of the Synanon Cult: The Managerial Strategy of Organizational Transformation' Synanon started as a voluntary association of former alcoholics, developed into a Therapeutic Community for substance dependent persons, transformed into a social movement or intentional society ending up as a cult propagating the 'Synanon religion or Synanon Church' (Ofshe, 1980).

Ultimately Synanon run into trouble with the US Internal Revenue Service lost its tax exempt status and was obliged to pay a very large sum of owed taxes which lead it to bankruptcy. Adding to the financial problems there were accusations hurled against it as being involved in 'criminal activities' and the organization was finally and formally dissolved in 1991.

For those of our readers wishing to have a more lengthy account of the birth, rise and demise of Synanon we suggest among other books Professor Rod Janzen's book titled: *'The Rise and Fall of Synanon, a California Utopia'* in which he notes that more than 25,000 people at various times were involved as members of Synanon among them artists and musicians. Indeed, large numbers of participants were indeed helped with their dependency problems while some of its most noted supporters were Senator Thomas Dodd, comedian Steve Allen and the psychologist Abraham Maslow, globally known for his *'hierarchy of human needs'* oftentime depicted in a pyramidal fashion (Janzen, 2001).

The **Therapeutic Community,** (TC) a residential, in-patient, long term treatment modality proliferated across the USA from the East Coast to the West Coast in the 1960's and the 1970's and was to some extent influenced by Synanon principles and practices. During that period many Therapeutic Communities were initiated, operated and staffed by paraprofessionals and recovered 'ex-addicts' and only a handful of TC's accepted and integrated in their staff a minute number of professionals such as social workers, psychologists and psychiatrists.

Therapeutic Communities of the sixties and seventies were described as 'concept' TC's which meant that they focused on the whole person and not just his or her success in abstinence from the use of drugs emphasizing the need for the individual's overall life-style change. Some of the therapeutic tools which originated with Synanon such as the intense, sometimes brutal, *'intake interview'*; going 'cold turkey' (which means ceasing to use heroin and opiates and detoxifying without the help of substitutes) in the first few days after admission; cutting all communication with family and friends for several weeks were broadly adopted by TC's with observable variations dictated by their founders in cooperation with the nucleus of their founding staff. Therapeutic Communities also adopted and tailored to their staff's philosophies and techniques of operation (giving it some other names) the so-called 'Synanon Game' where participants spoke about themselves using any and as many profanities as they wished and then receiving the brutal criticism, enriched by a plethora of profanities, from their peers.

In their early years of operation the vast majority of Therapeutic Communities expected that the time length of drug addicts as residents undergoing treatment ('junkies') should be 18 to 24 months and the progress of the individual was broadly tailored after Synanon's 3-stage progression of participants toward full recovery. The progression through the 3-stage program was adopted in most 'Concept' TC's. During the first stage residents are assigned the 'lowest possible roles' in the social hierarchy of the residential community which translates into doing basic chores and housekeeping duties; during the second stage, if they are judged as having been successful in their execution of first stage roles, residents are given higher level social roles and may be assigned (as team mates to qualified staff members) duties outside the program but they still reside and sleep in the facility; during the third stage residents are permitted to re-enter their communities, find employment or enrol in a 'second chance' high school if they have been 'drop-outs', secure living accommodation and reside outside the TC residential facility.

A 'drug-free' or 'concept' Therapeutic Community, also known as TC for addictions has been defined as 'a drug-free' total abstinence from the use of any form of drugs environment in which recovering addicted individuals and recovered 'ex-addicts' live in the same facility and work together in an organised and structured way. Participating in the TC life the residents work toward freeing themselves from self-destructive and anti-social styles of life. Going through rigorous and properly structured and carefully overseen resocialization processes the residents internalize values such as honesty, responsibility assumption, exhibiting desire to learn and attitude for hard work become re-socialized. Ultimately TC residents having negated their previous negative, anti-social and self-destructive life styles, evolve into responsible individuals aiming to carry on living a positive, socially acceptable drug-free life when reaching the third-stage of re-entrance to the outside society (De Leon and Ziegenfuss, 1986).

In the early history of TC's most residents were adult heroin users. By the late seventies half of the TC populations were heroin users and the other half were involved in the use of marijuana, hallucinogens, amphetamines and sedatives. In the middle eighties TC populations were primarily users of cocaine and crack cocaine. The 'Concept' Therapeutic Communities are now catering to large numbers of women and adolescents and have undergone significant changes in their staffing patterns incorporating large numbers of mental health professionals who work along with the classic 'ex-addict' paraprofessional personnel.

In Europe the same proliferation of TC's took place at about the same chronological period as various European Nations were encountering increased involvement of countless thousands of users especially in the use of heroin. Initially the American type of the Therapeutic Community modality, its fundamental philosophy, sociological structure and psychological strategies were copied across the European Nations. The European TC's adopted the American psychological concepts and techniques such as 'the encounter sessions' taking place at least 2-3 times per week and lasting up to two hours where residents were fiercely criticized for unacceptable behaviour and the once a month 'marathon encounter session' lasting 24 to 30 hours.

Eventually European TC's complemented the American behavioural treatment approach adding psychoanalytic thinking, educational theories, social learning and massive involvement of professionals in the TC structure in contrast to the original American style of large numbers of recovered e-addicts and limited numbers of professionals in staffing TC's. Following the 1990 collapse of the Union of Soviet Socialist Republics (USSR) many TC's appeared as a treatment modality in ex-communist Nations where large numbers of people used heroin and encountered problems as drug users (Vanderplasschen et al, EMCDDA 2014).

As we noted above Therapeutic Communities in the late sixties and seventies sprang up all over the United States as a response to dealing with the epidemic proportions of substance use especially heroin and other opiates and opioids. Nowadays the American model of 'concept' TC's has adapted to many new orientations in its structure, organization and staffing patterns and it is estimated that TC's currently exist in dozens of countries across the Globe. Indeed in most countries, as well as in the USA, TCs have abandoned their insistence on refusal to permit some residents take any type of drugs, time lengths of residency have been cut drastically and in the place of the 18-24 month residency requirements many TC's have adopted models of 3 to 6 and up to 12 months in-patient residency and participation in day-programs. Some evidence suggests that the longer the involvement of individuals in a TC the better are the outcomes. Contrary to the all adult TC population with limited participation of women with SUD's as was the case in the sixties and seventies, modern TC's cater to mixed populations, some specialize in serving adolescents and families providing a broad spectrum of special counselling, family counselling, and granting permission to attend schools (De Leon, 2000; Perfas and Spross, 2007).

PART FOUR - TOBACCO

Preamble

At the start of this fourth and final part of our book father and daughter as co-authors, decided to be candid and disclose to you our readers, what our relatives, friends, associates and ex-students have known all along: we both were but no longer are cigarette smokers. Georgios did not smoke a single cigarette while attending High School in Greece. He started smoking while he was an undergraduate in New York and continued smoking for the next 27 years having reached the level of smoking 2 packs a day. Natasha did not smoke a single cigarette while she was a High School student in Greece but she started smoking while she was a University student in the UK and continued to smoke for the next 8 years. Twenty seven years after he had started smoking in New York, not facing any health problems but simply motivated by the wish to 'liberate' himself from the habit of consuming more than two packs a day, Georgios spent 6 months of an agonizing struggle to stop smoking and get rid of his tobacco-nicotine dependence. Natasha admits that stopping her cigarette smoking was for her a much easier task compared to her father's agonizing efforts. She was emotionally helped and behaviourally motivated by the life changing discovery that she was pregnant carrying her son, (Georgios' grandson) Harry. Additionally, hormonal changes related with pregnancy and aversion to smoke and nicotine taste constituted further help in her ceasing to smoke cigarettes. Harry is a healthy teenager and a talented basketball player who abhors cigarettes and vaping. Both co-authors hope that you have noticed that this book is dedicated to Harry, Natasha's son and Georgios' grandson.

19 TOBACCO CHEWING & SMOKING

According to the Australian New South Wales Cancer Council, a non-profit, anti-smoking organization, tobacco has been growing wild in the Americas as far back as 8,000 years ago (around 6,000 BC). Humans started using it by chewing tobacco leaves during cultural or religious ceremonies and events at year 1 BC preceding the birth of Jesus by one year (New South Wales Cancer Council online; Randall, 1999). The same chronological period of 6,000 B.C. in reference to tobacco growing in North and South America is given online in an Atlas presented by the World Health Organization (WHO) as a pdf (Mackay and Eriksen 2002).

The consensus of academic sources and Mass Media of Communication references is that tobacco was first encountered by Europeans in 1492 when Christopher Columbus and his crew set foot on the shores of the New World. The Spanish explorers observed indigenous people, in the new Western hemisphere world they had just discovered, chewing the leaves or taking puffs from slowly burning dark brown plant leaves. The plant leaves were rolled into a pipe shape which they placed in their mouths, inhaled and then exhaled smoke from their mouths and their nostrils. Be it as it may, at the end of the 15th century Europeans came to know a natural plant named tobacco. Tobacco is the popular, common name for several dozens of similar plants belonging to the *Nicotiana* family which originally grew in the Americas and after their discovery by Columbus in the last few centuries have been cultivated and used in the form of chewing or smoking their leaves in most parts of the world. Tobacco leaves contain, among other substances, the stimulant alkaloid *nicotine* which constitutes a highly addictive substance responsible for creating tobacco-addiction (NIDA January 2020).

Samples of those plant leaves, samples of tobacco, were brought back initially to Spain and introduced to the European continent during the end of the 15th and with increased frequency during the 16th century when tobacco smoking spread across to England and to other European Nations. According to the WHO Atlas presenting the history and spread of tobacco the Turks introduced tobacco to Egypt and during the 16th century Portuguese and Spaniards introduced tobacco to East Africa. From there tobacco use spread to the West and South parts of the African continent. During the 16th and 17th centuries' tobacco was introduced by Japan and the Philippines to India and China (where it spread quickly engulfing large numbers of the population). By the 18th century tobacco smoking had become quite widespread in Europe and USA and a tobacco industry was formed (WHO Tobacco Atlas).

On a global scale, over 1.1 billion people were reported as smokers in 2014 and the number has not been significantly lowered in 2020. Among tobacco users, with a ratio of 4 to 1, men smokers outnumber women smokers. The dramatic and dangerous aspects of using tobacco products is exemplified by the fact that over 8 million persons died in 2017 from causes related to this habit. This statistic has an even more impressively dramatic characteristic as it is reported that 7 million of those lost their lives because they smoked and over 1.2 million died, although they were non-smokers or users, simply because they were exposed to second-hand smoke. It is calculated that tobacco smoking ultimately kills half of its users and the estimates are that during the span of the 20th century over 100 million deaths were attributed to smoking tobacco (WHO July 26, 2019).

In the last few decades, recognizing the high number of deaths and the escalating costs of treating ailments related to tobacco smoking, on a global scale Central Governments along with Regional and municipal authorities, Charitable Institutions, families and individuals have been involved in concerted efforts to curtail the tobacco using habits. In this respect, imposition of high taxes and levies on tobacco products along with statutes prohibiting smoking in enclosed public places, in closed quarters such as company and public service offices, restaurants, bars, coffee shops and bus, train and airport terminals appear to be helping. The ban on smoking on buses and railroad trains as well as in airplanes during national and international flights has surely benefited the 'passive smokers' from tobacco's catastrophic effects. Additional help in the fight against tobacco uses comes from prohibitions in advertising tobacco products and from systematic campaigns which point to the real health hazards of smoking as for example from the Centers for Disease Control and Prevention (CDC), a major operating component of the US Department of Health and Human Services (CDC About the Campaign).

Furthermore, restrictions on curbing the marketing appeal of using combinations of colours and designs of hard and soft cigarette packages and warnings printed on packages such as 'cigarettes can seriously damage your health' or more blunt ones such as 'smoking kills' are widely used across the Globe and they, along with prohibition of selling cigarettes to minors, seem to be strengthening the global efforts aiming to curtail the smoking habit and save lives.

However, despite the fact that efforts aimed to control and curtail tobacco consumption on a global scale are liberating many persons from their nicotine addiction, at the same time the rising numbers of global populations result in impressive increases in the quantities of cigarettes, cigars, pipe and tobacco for self-roll cigarettes consumed every year. Counting over 1.1 billion smokers remains a serious challenge to humanity from a hazardous habit which during most of the 20th century was considered as 'glamorous and cool behaviour' for both men and women.

With the onset of the 20th century cigarettes, cigars, pipes and the *hookah* (also known with the Turkish name *nargile* where it was widely used for several centuries) became a prominent fad and smoking became a fashionable type of behaviour. The pipes for smoking tobacco are made of a variety of materials ranging from wood to metal and they consist of a little bowl where tobacco is placed and a pipe which the smokers hold in their hand and place in their mouths for taking a puff. The hookah, or nargile, is made of a variety of materials, comes in a variety of shapes and consists of the body which is a glass bottle usually half-filled with water, a long flexible haul which connects the smoker to the bottle, and a small cup on the top where the tobacco is placed. On some types of nargile or hookah several hoses each with its own mouthpiece can be adopted so that more than one person can smoke from the same apparatus.

As Phil Edwards has noted in his April 6, 2015 article in the VOX titled '*What everyone gets wrong about the history of cigarettes*' up to 1880 skilled tobacco workers were hand-rolling cigarettes at rates of a few per minute. In 1880 James Bonsack invented a machine capable of producing 210 cigarettes per minute or some 200,000 in 10 operating hours. James Buchanan Duke's American Tobacco Company adopted Bonsack's machine and revolutionized both the production and the consumption of cigarettes. The innovative Bonsack's machine produced very long cigarettes which were cut by fast moving blades to the usual length of appx 84mm for regular or 100mm for the so-called 100's. As time passed, improvements on the original cigarette producing machinery and new inventions gave to the Tobacco Industries tremendous impetus for very large scale production of lowered cost quantities and sale of cigarettes for huge profits (Edwards, P., Vox.com, 2015), (Kremer, W. BBC 2012), (Cross, G and Proctor, R., 2014).

The introduction of machinery producing large quantities of cigarettes created the unexpected problem of having larger supplies than were demanded by smokers. The tobacco industries did engage in wide advertising campaigns to create appropriate level demand for their product and did succeed in creating demand as more and more people were attracted to this new behaviour and started to smoke. Enhanced marketing efforts promoting the uses of cigarettes, cigars and other tobacco products spread across the globe. It should be noted that the Tobacco Industries provided soldiers with cigarettes, given along with their rations to serve as stress and emotional tensions reducers during both WWI and WWII (Smith, E.A. & Malone, R.E., 2009).

As a teenager growing up in Greece in the 1950's and a freshman foreign student in 1960 at CCNY (of the City University of New York), Georgios the 'senior' co-author (senior in age not in the contribution to the creation of this e-book) can recall Hollywood films portraying images of male stars such as, among others, the Americans James Dean, Humphrey Bogart and the Frenchman Jean-Paul Belmondo making smoking 'look cool'. At the same time female stars like, among others, Marlene Dietrich, Lauren Bacall and Audrey Hepburn portrayed with subtle sexual innuendos the glamour and sophistication characterizing women who smoke cigarettes.

In New York city Georgios saw, as countless other millions of New Yorkers and visitors to the City, and was immensely impressed by the gigantic billboard of Camel cigarettes on the East side of Broadway between 43 and 44th Streets which rhythmically and in set time intervals exhaled huge puffs of tobacco smoke. That Billboard and many other conceptually similar marketing devices promoting the use of tobacco products were removed from public display.

Relevant to Georgios' experience with the 'Camel Man' is the opening paragraph of Alan M. Brandt's book (2007), a Pulitzer Prize finalist titled '*The Cigarette Century*' where he writes: "*In 1961 when I was 7 years old my parents took me to New York City for the first time. In this, my introduction to the City's many sights and attractions, nothing elicited my attention and fascination more than the famous Camel billboard looming over Times Square. The Camel Man blew endless perfect smoke rings into the neon-lit night sky. I was quite simply amazed…*" (p.1)

Current news Reports appearing regularly in the Mass Media emphasize the trend that smoking is associated more with middle and low income persons and on a global scale is less prevalent in industrially developed and financially advanced Nations and more so in less industrialized and economically developed Nations. Indeed according to the World Health Organization's (WHO) report mentioned earlier, of the 1.1 billion smokers worldwide 80% live in low-and-middle-income countries where the burdens of tobacco-related illness and deaths are the heaviest. In these countries, as is the case also with low income smokers who live in richer countries, money wasted on buying tobacco and satisfying the addictive habit limits the low available financial resources needed to buy food and other necessities and secure shelter.

Both co-authors of the book you are reading (and both '*ex-smokers*') we confess in all honesty, that despite the fact that we are aware of this reality as we observe it on a daily basis, we were really dismayed reading in the **Independent** on 31 May, 2018 an article signed by Oliver Smith placing our homeland Greece on the 12th highest position in a scale of smoking among the World's Nations. In the same article the USA, where Georgios begun to smoke, is placed at the 68th position while the UK where Natasha studied and where she first learned how to smoke is placed at the 79th position (Smith, O., 2018).

The statistics for Greece paint a more negative reality as in the World atlas (accessible on line), according to data provided by the World Health Organization and CIA fact book our homeland Greece is placed in the 3rd place worldwide as 42.4% of the country's adults continue to smoke. According to this Report the top ten countries where significant portions of their adult population are smokers in descending order are: 1. Kiribati (52.2%), 2. Nauru (47.5%), 3. Greece (42.4%), 4. Serbia (41.6%), 5. Jordan (41%), 6. Indonesia (39.8%), 7. Russia (39.1%), 8.Lebanon (38.3%), 9. Bosnia and Herzegovina (38.3%), 10.Chile (38%) (Wee, Rolando Y., 2018).

The impressive current statistic of 1.1 Tobacco users on a global scale should be enhanced by some equally impressive statistics of the tobacco industry revenues. A brief report of the British American Tobacco Company (BAT) indicates that the global tobacco market in 2017 generated US$785 billion (excluding revenues generated in China). More than $700 billion of this amount came from the sale of some 5,400 billion cigarettes. Estimates are that the vaping e-cigarettes market generates over US$18 billion and the oral tobacco and nicotine market another US$ 12.5 billion (British American Tobacco., BAT, the global market).

20 VAPING E-CIGARETTES

Vaping devices, also known as 'e-cigarettes', according to the relevant on-line report of the US National Institute on Drug Abuse, are battery operated, hand held devices used to imitate the tobacco smoking ritual. Individuals use them to inhale an aerosol usually containing a variety of chemicals and flavorings in liquid form such as propylene glycol, glycerin, flavorings or other liquids and if chosen by the user liquid nicotine. These devices resemble traditional size cigarettes, cigars, pipes or a variety of other shapes and forms. When they are larger, also hand held, they carry a small refillable tank where the user, the 'vaper', can pour one of the more than 460 e-cigarette liquid brands available globally (NIDA January 2020).

A variety of references exist relating to the timing of the invention, production and sales of e-cigarettes. CASAA (Consumer Advocates for Smoke free Alternatives Association, a totally volunteer, non- profit organization based in Plattsburg, New York) offers a historical outline on e-cigarettes from the 1930's to our times. According to the CASAA a Chinese pharmacist, inventor and smoker named Hon Lik, a 3-pack a day cigarette smoker who had lost his father, also a heavy smoker, from tobacco caused cancer and the company he worked for Golden Dragon Holdings based in Beijing are credited with the discovery and public sale of the first commercially successful e-cigarettes in 2003. According to CASAA's timetable e-cigarettes were introduced to Europe in 2006, to the USA in 2007 and are now globally available as alternatives to smoking tobacco (CASAA, historical timeline for electronic cigarettes).

A special World Health Organization report titled *'Marketers of electronic cigarettes should halt unproved therapy claims'* and published in Geneva on September 19, 2008 stated: *'Contrary to what some marketers of the electronic cigarette imply in their advertisements, the World Health Organization (WHO) does not consider it to be a legitimate therapy for smokers trying to quit'* (WHO 19 September, 2008).

Despite warnings from National and International Health Agencies the number of vaper using e-cigarettes, as Lora Jones reported on September 15, 2019 in a BBC Business News story, has risen globally from about 7 million in 2011 to over 41 million in 2018. In the article it is noted that the global market is estimated to be worth $19.3bn (£15.5bn), up from $6.9bn (£5.5bn) just five years ago. Three countries are the biggest markets: the USA, The UK and France where more than $10bn (£8bn) were spent on smokeless tobacco and vaping products in 2018 (Jones, BBC News 15 September 2019).

Michael Standaert reporting in the Guardian on December 1, 2018 under the title '*Shenzhen, vaping capital of the world, holds its breath as health concerns spiral*' noted that in this city just north of Hong Kong the Chinese employ more than two million workers in about 1,000 factories and the relevant cluster of supply-chain SME's and produce almost 90% of the World's vaping and e-cigarette devices (Standaert, December 1, 2019).

A fairly extensive September 15, 2019 Special Report in the Guardian signed by Jamie Doward and titled '*After six deaths in the US and bans around the world – is vaping safe?*' raises more questions as it answers some fundamental ones relating to evidence on vaping-e-cigarettes being or not bring hazardous to users' health. The Report points out the conflicting stand of UK Authorities as on the one hand they admit that there are dangers in vaping since there are no conclusive longitudinal studies characterizing it 'health-hazard-free' while, on the other hand, bringing forth the Nation's concern with the existing seven million tobacco smokers. In the same Report an interesting note is made by Dr Simon Capewell, professor of clinical epidemiology at Liverpool University when, commenting on how the tobacco industry is handling the rising popularity of vaping e-cigarettes, he laconically commented: '*What is the tobacco industry doing? Buying up electronic cigarette companies as fast as it can and pushing vaping very hard...*' (Doward, September 15, 2019).

Prompted by the above statement by Professor Capewell we suggest you take a look at the bold position against vaping e-cigarettes and the dangers associated with them he took in his article published in the Mail-on-line on June,17 and updated June 18, 2019 bearing the alarming title: '*Toxic reality of trendy 'harmless' e-cigarettes: Professor of clinical epidemiology SIMON CAPEWELL says there's growing evidence that vaping may damage the lungs, heart or brain*' (Capewell, June 17 and 18, 2019).

The American Cancer Society in a 2018 statement took a clear stand suggesting that no young persons should start using tobacco products including e-cigarettes. Indeed the ACS clearly states that as far as tobacco smokers are concerned 'e-cigarettes should not be used to quit smoking as a cessation method' (American Cancer Society February 2018).

In news reports published in the summer of 2019 by a variety of News Media such as the German News Agency DW, European Union's Euro-News and others it was made public that the UN Health Agency World Health Organization considers e-cigarettes '*undoubtedly harmful and despite their producers marketing statements they do not help people quit tobacco smoking*' (DW.com July 26, 2019; Bosqued Riera, euronews.com July 31, 2019).

Having disclosed earlier that both co-authors of this book are 'ex-smokers' of cigarettes, we feel obliged to explain why we discuss vaping e-cigarettes here, right after our discussion on smoking tobacco, instead of doing so in the section on treating nicotine addiction and the smoking habit which will follow. As persons who underwent the agonizing processes and experienced the relevant trials and tribulations on our road to recovery until we were freed from our smoking habit and nicotine addiction, we feel that vaping e-cigarettes is not exactly an appropriate method for successfully 'kicking-off' this debilitating habit. Our belief is based on the observable realities that the process of vaping e-cigarettes carries a number of 'addictive' experiences associated with and relating to the ritual of lighting and smoking a tobacco cigarette, a cigar or even a pipe, inhaling and then ritually exhaling smoke from the mouth and the nostrils.

In all of the above instances the ritual commences and progresses with the extraction of a cigarette from its package, playing it for a short while in the fingers, placing it in the mouth, light it and take the first deep puff and then exhale smoke from the mouth and the nostrils. It was these motions of hand to mouth, inhaling a puff and exhaling smoke, this musculoskeletal ritual of movements as we experienced while liberating ourselves from the smoking-habit-nicotine-addiction that were especially difficult to overcome. Vaping e-cigarettes encompasses all these motions, the whole ritual, and in essence enhances, it does not weaken the smoking habit.

21 THE ROAD TO NICOTINE ADDICTION

Parents, adolescents and other members of the general public concerned with the pervasive realities and statistics on tobacco smoking and smokeless tobacco consumption such as chewing will, when the occasion arises, pose the question to addiction experts: '*Is nicotine addictive?*'. The answer they will receive each and every time from each and every addiction expert will be an emphatic: YES! Most tobacco users are 'hooked' on smoking cigarettes, cigars and pipes as well as smoking 'self-roll' tobacco cigarettes (falsely thinking they are less harmful) and those who chew tobacco do so because they are addicted to the nicotine contained in tobacco leaves.

Most smokers will admit that they tried their first cigarette while they were adolescents a fact which raises serious questions as sale of tobacco, as a rule, is forbidden to minors. In this respect as an eloquent answer the adage that 'all rules have their exceptions' comes in mind. The vast majority of adolescents learn to smoke when they join a group of peers where some members are already smokers and they introduce them to the cigarette smoking ritual. Some teenagers start to smoke when they enter a romantic affair with a person who smokes. A very limited number of adolescents begin to smoke on their own and without appropriate reinforcing stimuli they do not continue their self-learned smoking habit for long.

In an extensive meta-analysis which included 75 longitudinal studies across 16 countries published in the Psychological Bulletin, (issue 10, vol. 143 in October 2017), titled: '*The Influence of Peer Behavior as a Function of Social and Cultural Closeness: A Meta-Analysis of Normative Influence on Adolescent Smoking Initiation and Continuation*' the authors note that (a) smoking initiation was more positively correlated with peers' smoking when the interpersonal closeness between adolescents and their peers was higher (vs. lower); and (b) both smoking initiation and continuation were more positively correlated with peers' smoking when samples were from collectivistic (vs. individualistic) cultures (Jiaying Liu, Siman Zhao, Xi Chen, Emily Falk, Dolores Albarracín, 2017).

The classic interpretive etiological model and relevant understanding during the 20th century was that people do not become nicotine addicts by smoking one or two cigarettes or after they have used one or two packs of cigarettes or have chewed a few small patches of tobacco.

This perception seems to be refuted by recent studies. Specifically in a study which monitored 1,246 sixth-grade students in six Massachusetts communities over four years conducted by the University of Massachusetts Medical School, Joseph R. Difranza, MD, professor of family medicine & community health at the University of Massachusetts Medical School and leader of the UMMS research team commented that *'Laboratory experiments confirm that nicotine alters the structure and function of the brain within a day of the very first dose. In humans, nicotine-induced alterations in the brain can trigger addiction with the first cigarette'* (Difranza, J.R., 2007).

A more recent study, titled: *'What Proportion of People Who Try One Cigarette Become Daily Smokers? A Meta-Analysis of Representative Surveys'* and published in the Nicotine and Tobacco Research Journal in 2018 was widely covered by the Mass Media as it focused on 8 international surveys conducted between 2000 and 2016 in which 216,314 respondents were included. Of the 8 surveys, 3 were conducted in the USA, 3 in the UK and one each in Australia and New Zealand. The surveys study created a significant stir as it concluded that: *'Over two-thirds of people who try one cigarette become, at least temporarily, daily smokers'* (Birge, M., Duffy, S., Miler, J. A., Hajek, P., 2018).

We suggest to our readers who wish to gain a better perspective and a more thorough understanding of what the nicotine addiction as well as the liberation from this addiction entail to read at an excellent and extensive relevant report of the US National Institute on Drug Abuse accessible free on line titled *'Tobacco, Nicotine and E-Cigarettes'* (NIDA January 2020).

According to this NIDA Report revised in November 2019 *'A transient surge of endorphins in the reward circuits of the brain causes a slight, brief euphoria when nicotine is administered. This surge is much briefer than the "high" associated with other drugs but like other drugs of abuse, nicotine increases levels of the neurotransmitter dopamine in these reward circuits'* (Picciotto and Mineur, 2013; Balfour DJK, 2015).

Jackson, Muldoon, De Biasi and Damaj, in their Neuropharmacology Journal article bearing the title *'New mechanisms and perspectives in nicotine withdrawal'* have noted that when cigarette smoke enters the lungs, nicotine is absorbed rapidly in the blood and delivered quickly to the brain, so that nicotine levels peak within 10 seconds of inhalation. But the acute effects of nicotine also dissipate quickly, along with the associated feelings of reward; this rapid cycle causes the smoker to continue dosing to maintain the drug's pleasurable effects and prevent withdrawal symptoms (Jackson et al., 2015).

Each and every year countless numbers of the over 1.1 billion smokers all over the globe including those living in North America and European countries, make honest attempts to quit smoking but apparently only a small percentage succeed in their efforts. In an online report published in 2019 by the US Food and Drug Administration titled: *'Quitting Smoking: Closer with Every Attempt'* it is noted that in 2015 only 7% were successful in quitting for a period of 6-12 months (US FDA December 31, 2019). Although the specific data refer to the experiences of American smokers we can fairly safely assume that matters are not very different but more or less similar on a global scale.

The real statistics bring to our minds the quote attributed to the famous American author Samuel Clemens known worldwide as 'Mark Twain' and his serious addiction almost from his childhood years to cigar smoking. In a presentation by Alejandro Benes from an article written by Tom Selleck in the magazine *'Cigar Aficionado'*, winter 1995-1996 issue, titled: 'Samuel Clemens and His Cigars - Samuel Clemens, AKA Mark Twain, found his muse in great plumes of cigar smoke' we read that Clemens tried to quit or cut back on his massive consumption of cigars, but he just couldn't manage it. *"To cease smoking is the easiest thing. I ought to know. I've done it a thousand times"* (Benes, A. from Selleck, T. cigar aficionado).

Individuals should realize that they are addicted to nicotine when, as noted below, they experience symptoms like the following while attempting to stop smoking or curtail the number of cigarettes they consume. The current edition of the American Psychiatric Association's Diagnostic Statistical Manual (DSM-5) uses the term *tobacco use disorder* which replaced the term *nicotine addiction* used in the previous edition (DSM-4) highlighting that:

- You can't stop smoking. You've made one or more serious, but unsuccessful, attempts to stop.
- You experience withdrawal symptoms when you try to stop. Your attempts at stopping have caused physical and mood-related symptoms, such as strong cravings, anxiety, irritability, restlessness, difficulty concentrating, depressed mood, frustration, anger, increased hunger, insomnia, constipation or diarrhoea.
- You keep smoking despite health problems. Even though you've developed health problems with your lungs or your heart, you haven't been able to stop.
- You give up social or recreational activities in order to smoke. You may stop going to smoke-free restaurants or stop socializing with certain family members or friends because you can't smoke in these locations or situations (Mayo Clinic online: Nicotine Dependence).

22 THE ROAD TO RECOVERY FROM NICOTINE ADDICTION

Nicotine addiction encompasses a number of specific pharmacological, psychological and social characteristics which bind the smokers to their habit giving the dimensions of a colossal task requiring Herculean efforts to their attempts to 'free' themselves. Matters become even more perplexed with the condition of smoking as the existing and verified effects on the smokers health, such as the threat of lung cancer and a number of other health dangers is not perceived as an immediate, eminently present danger. A minimal number of smokers manage to dissociate themselves from their nicotine addiction while the vast majority will use combinations of NRT (Nicotine Replacement Therapy) products, psycho-therapeutic support and counselling. The NRT products will cover the smokers' bodily-pharmacological needs while psychotherapy and counselling will assist them in really 'breaking the chains' holding them attached to smoking.

If you are currently a 'smoker' or if you are an 'ex-smoker' you will understand what Samuel Clemens, also known as Mark Twain, meant as you will recognize that the smoking ritual entails many specific and pleasure producing characteristics. One of the various 'addiction enhancing characteristics' relating to the habitual smoking is that smokers will light a cigarette as a response when finding themselves in a variety of contrasting types of emotions and stages of moods. In real life terms, smokers will light a cigarette to celebrate and enhance an elated emotional and mood stage when an accomplishment is achieved or a goal is reached. In the diametrically exact opposite case of low emotional and mood stage, smokers will 'console' themselves by lighting a cigarette when things have not gone as expected and goal achievement or task completion has been frustrated!

Emphasizing the above description of explaining attachment to the smoking habit we can say that smokers will smoke because they feel 'high' and they will smoke because they feel 'low'.

Addiction to *nicotine,* the highly addictive substance contained in the tobacco products you use as packaged or 'self-rolling' cigarettes, cigars, pipes or chewable tobacco leaf patches, can be cured by using a variety of means which include behavioral treatment therapy and special nicotine replacement therapy (NRT) products. In many cases a proper combination of both psychotherapeutic support and NRT products increase considerably the rates of success in quitting (Stead LF, Koilpillai P, Fanshawe TR, Lancaster T. 2016)

Psychological help to smokers actively engaged and motivated to free themselves from their nicotine addiction entails a number of sessions in Cognitive Behavioral Therapy (CBT). This type of psychotherapy, as we presented it earlier in this book, focuses on the smokers' current realities and less on issues of their past. Refreshing our readers' memory of the strategy and techniques CBT entails, we will note here the assumption made by CBT therapists that our actions, physical sensations, thoughts and feelings are dynamically interconnected and in pathological cases, such as the smokers' addiction to nicotine, are the result of being trapped in behavioral vicious cycles. In the number of CBT sessions designed as appropriate to each individual the smokers are helped to identify the negative triggers influencing their behavior, i.e. thoughts, feelings, persons, activities and replace them with positive ones which will free them from reliance on the use of tobacco products in dealing with daily life and work difficulties.

In the USA in applying Nicotine Replacement Therapy (NRT), several nicotine replacement products are approved by the FDA. In a similar fashion in the UK several NRT products have been approved and are often provided through the National Health Systems (NHS) in the form of free prescriptions while some European Union Nations also permit selective usage. Our advice to our readers is that smokers interested in using NRT products should consult the National Drug Administration Authorities of their own country noting that in all European Union member States they can receive relevant and authoritative information from medical personnel as well as pharmacies and pharmacists properly licensed to operate in each of the 27 EU member States.

Nicotine Replacement Therapy (NRT) products come in a variety of forms as shown below:

The *nicotine patch. This is a transdermal patch produced by more than one pharmaceutical companies and is available at potencies of 5mg, 10mg and 15mg or 7mg, 14 mg and 21 mg to be used in a 24 hour period and come under brand names such as NiQuitin or Nicorette.*

   The *nicotine chewing gum. The gum comes in potencies of 2mg or 4mg.*

   The *nicotine lozenges. They come in potencies of 1mg as well as 2mg and 4 mg.*

   The *nicotine nasal spray. This comes in potency of 0.5gr with each dose.*

   The *nicotine inhaler. This comes in potency of 10 mg as an inhalation cartage & mouth piece.*

Beyond the above Nicotine Replacement Therapy (NRT) products Bupropion and Varenicline are two other approved medical products which can be used in the process of helping smokers overcome their nicotine addiction.

Bupropion was originally used as an antidepressant and is usually marketed in two forms, namely as an immediate release form and an extended release form and according to some relevant studies appears to bolster the rates of recovery of smokers from nicotine addiction.

Varenicline manages to reduce nicotine cravings by acting as a partial agonist stimulating the alpha-4 and beta-2 nicotinic acetylcholine receptors but less intensely than nicotine does. In relevant studies Verenicline combined with Cognitive Behavioral Therapy sessions appears to give better results than NRT products and Bupropion used alone (Aubin H-J, et al, 2014; Hughes JR, et al 2014).

A relatively new approach in the treatment of addictions is the Transcranial Magnetic Stimulation (TMS) a physiological intervention that noninvasively stimulates neural activity in targeted areas of the brain using magnetic fields. Although the approach is new some initial work with smokers engaged in freeing themselves from nicotine addiction appears to have provided some promising results (Dinur-Klein L, et al 2014).

23 'SMIRTING': SMOKING BANS CREATE A NOVEL SOCIO-PSYCHOLOGICAL PHENOMENON

In closing PART FOUR of our book which dealt with the issues of smoking and vaping, we feel obliged to make a brief mention of 'smirting' the peculiar socio-psychological phenomenon emerging as a by-product of imposing smoking bans in enclosed public places such as bars, pubs and cafes. 'Smirting' is a term emerging from the combination of the verbs 'smoking' and 'flirting'. It describes an unforeseen psycho-social reality by the imposition of smoking bans on Bars and Pubs where smokers walk out of the Bar or the Pub and while standing at the entrance of the drinking establishments they light and enjoy their cigarettes. In this type of unstructured gathering, smokers who did not belong to the same group of friends when they walked into the Bar or the Pub, or were not in close physical proximity while they were enjoying themselves in the Bar or the Pub, find themselves close to one another 'sharing' their 'condition' and socializing with other 'victims' of the smoking ban.

The Mass Media covered widely the new phenomenon of 'smirting' and many tickling 'confessions' were made to journalists as to significantly increased chances of flirting with others with who the smokers never thought would be able to socialize inside the Bar or the Pub (Cummins, N., 2004; Hughes, S., 2005; Lister, D., 2006; Evans, K., 2007; McGurk, J., 2007).

A number of Greek Governments had passed smoking bans in closed public places as bars, pubs and cafes several years ago but in reality those bans were not properly enforced most of the time. We have mentioned above the statistical facts describing the dramatic levels of smoking habits of our compatriots Greeks which were not helped to improve by the rampant leniency of permitting smoking in enclosed public places. The new National Government which was formed after the National Parliamentary election of the summer of 2019, has been systematically enforcing the anti-smoking bans and heavy fines have been imposed on businesses breaking the law. Interestingly enough what we described above as the 'smirting' phenomenon which first occurred in Ireland after the imposition of the relevant anti-smoking bans in that country is now becoming a socio-psychological reality in our homeland (Kampouris, N. 2019).

Be that as it may, we do hope that our readers will excuse us as we make the honest and frank statement that as 'ex-smokers', father and daughter as co-authors, each and every time we see those 'smirting' outside bars, cafes and pubs defying the weather conditions and while trembling from the winter cold, getting wet from the drizzle or suffering the summer heat outside the enclosed air conditioned halls of Bars and Pubs, we do smile with sincere 'empathy' and we do make an honest wish that someday they will find the will needed and while supported from family, friends and professional helpers they will free themselves from their smoking 'condition'.

Georgios had written a brief comment on 'smirting' in 2011, reproduced widely in Greek blogs, sites and Mass Media which, in a poetic sense sprinkled with some caustic irony posed the naïve question: *'If the flirt blossoms into a full-fledge love affair for some men and women of those engaging in the new 'smirting' phenomena, will they decide to get cured of their smoking dependency and proceed hand in hand on the road to nicotine addiction recovery, free of their debilitating smoking habit, or will they choose to hide their romance in the combined clouds of tobacco smoke as they light their next cigarettes?'* (Piperopoulos, G., 2011, Greek text).

Printed in the USA
CPSIA information can be obtained
at www.ICGtesting.com
LVHW021523200624
783545LV00013B/552